HAWAII

By William Graves, *Senior Editorial Staff*
With Illustrations by James L. Amos, *Staff Photographer*
Foreword by Gilbert M. Grosvenor, *Associate Editor*
Produced by the Special Publications Division, Robert L. Breeden, *Chief*
National Geographic Society, Washington, D. C.
Melvin M. Payne, *President*
Melville Bell Grosvenor, *Editor-in-Chief*
Frederick G. Vosburgh, *Editor*

HAWAII

By WILLIAM GRAVES,
National Geographic Senior Editorial Staff
Photographs by JAMES L. AMOS,
National Geographic Photographer

Published by
THE NATIONAL GEOGRAPHIC SOCIETY
MELVIN M. PAYNE, *President*
MELVILLE BELL GROSVENOR, *Editor-in-Chief*
FREDERICK G. VOSBURGH, *Editor*
GILBERT M. GROSVENOR, *Executive Editor for this series*
ROBERT L. CONLY, *Consulting Editor*

Prepared by
THE SPECIAL PUBLICATIONS DIVISION
ROBERT L. BREEDEN, *Editor*
DONALD J. CRUMP, *Associate Editor*
PHILIP B. SILCOTT, *Manuscript Editor*
JOHANNA G. FARREN, *Research and Style*
HELGA R. KOHL, *Research Assistant*
Illustrations
DAVID R. BRIDGE, *Picture Editor*
JOSEPH A. TANEY, *Art Director*
JOSEPHINE B. BOLT, *Assistant Art Director*
JOHANNA G. FARREN, RONALD M. FISHER, LOUISE GRAVES, H. ROBERT MORRISON, *Picture Legends*
PENELOPE W. SPRINGER, *Picture-Legend Research*
WILLIAM M. ALLAN, BOBBY G. CROCKETT, JOHN D. GARST, JR., MONICA T. WOODBRIDGE, ALFRED L. ZEBARTH, *Map Research and Production*
Production and Printing
ROBERT W. MESSER, *Production Manager*
ANN H. CROUCH, *Production Assistant*
JAMES R. WHITNEY, JOHN R. METCALFE, *Engraving and Printing*
CONSTANCE D. BROWN, SUZANNE J. JACOBSON, JOAN PERRY, DONNA C. REY, SANDRA A. TURNER, *Staff Assistants*
ANNE McCAIN, TONI WARNER, *Index*

Ceaseless surf washes glassy obsidian on Black Sand Beach near Kalapana on the "Big Island" of Hawaii. Overleaf: "Below is the cluster of islands floating on the sea.... Pointing to the rising rays of the sun." A mele, or poetic form of history recited through generations, paints a word portrait of Molokai (foreground) and Hawaii (far right background) with Lanai (right) and Maui (left) lying between. Page 1: An adaptation of the Kingdom of Hawaii's seal proclaims the state's motto: "The life of the land is perpetuated in righteousness."

DAVID R. BRIDGE, N.G.S. STAFF (RIGHT); OVERLEAF AND PAGE 1: N.G.S. PHOTOGRAPHER JAMES L. AMOS

FOREWORD

LIKE MANY ANOTHER MALIHINI—as Hawaiians warmly call a stranger— I had always imagined America's mid-Pacific outpost purely as a vacationist's paradise. I had conjured visions of aquamarine seas, vast stretches of coral beach, stately coconut palms, and equally stately Polynesians for whom life was a sort of endless luau.

The United States Army gave me quite a different view of the islands. In 1955 I was stationed in Honolulu with a psychological-warfare unit studying problems of communication between Americans and Asians in the Far East. Hawaii proved to be the perfect classroom.

For nearly two centuries the islands have formed a bridge between East and West, offering a case study in communication and understanding among widely different peoples. With an endless variety of races and cultures packed into a comparatively small area, Hawaiians long ago learned the vital lessons of tolerance and mutual respect. It is no accident that their land has suffered relatively little of the violence common in our world today, or that the Constitution of the 50th State begins with the gentle preamble: "We, the people of the State of Hawaii...with an understanding heart toward all the peoples of the earth...."

This book conveys that feeling. For months author Bill Graves and photographer Jim Amos traveled the Aloha State, and everywhere they went they encountered a genuine aloha spirit among people as diverse and warmhearted as any in the world.

Today many changes are overtaking Hawaii's bewitching islands. As more and more tourists discover them, developers clash with conservationists over dwindling scenic beauty. Pressure is enormous; by the year 1978 Hawaii expects 3,000,000 annual tourists—a number more than four times greater than its current permanent population of 700,000.

Recently I had a very personal view of change in the islands. While visiting Honolulu I tried to find the small house I had rented during my Army days only to discover that my bungalow had been displaced, along with a dozen neighbors, by a soaring high-rise apartment house.

Along a favorite surfing beach I found young Hawaiians riding boards shorter and lighter than the ones I had learned to use. A quick run convinced me they are easier to handle—but more difficult to paddle out into the long rollers. Or was it difficult because I was 15 years older? Though the boards may change, and the surfers may age, I am sure succeeding generations will continue to enjoy Hawaii's incomparable waves.

There is much more that is incomparable about our 50th State, with its majesty, its problems, its traditions. Bill Graves and Jim Amos have captured it all, in a brilliant text and in unforgettable photographs. Whether you are a *malihini* or a *kama'aina,* an old Hawaii hand, you will find much that is familiar and a good many surprises as well.

As the Hawaiians say, *Hele me ka hau'oli*—"Go with joy."

GILBERT M. GROSVENOR

9028

Erosion-scarred cliffs of Kauai's Na Pali Coast soar thousands of feet above the

mists and ʻōhiʻa-lehua *trees of Kalalau Valley.*

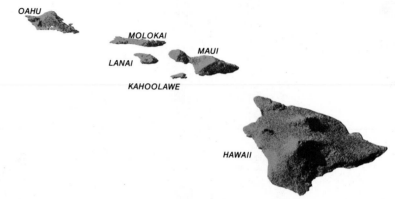

NIIHAU KAUAI OAHU MOLOKAI MAUI LANAI KAHOOLAWE HAWAII

THE ORIGIN

Islands shaped by fire, and children born of the sea

THROUGH THE VIOLET GLOOM 160 feet under the sea, giant spheres of stone take shape beneath us. We descend to the ocean floor as though entering a vast plaza whose cobbled surface lies bathed in eternal shadow.

Slowly, for I am new to such depths, I follow my diving partner Jim Robinson down the last few feet to the bottom. Nothing stirs at our approach. As we glide among the great stones, no cheerful clouds of reef fish wheel and dart before us in glittering escort. No *langouste* and moray peer from dark crevices, no albacore and bonito warily patrol the edges of the twilight. Here and there a starfish, its red-brown color transformed to iridescent green by an illusion of the depths, glistens like some fragment of wine bottle shattered on the stones.

Such desolation would mark the ordinary dive as a failure, but Jim and I are delighted. We have come not in search of marine life but to study the spheres themselves and the history of the great range of sea mountains called Hawaii. For the spheres are basalt, literally the birthstone of volcanic islands and the basic substance from which the 50th State was created. In exactly this form, though at *(Continued on page 16)*

Glowering temple image, a museum piece now, once evoked Hawaii's gods. Settled by Polynesians, discovered by Capt. James Cook, shepherded into the modern world by missionaries, Hawaii retains its pristine beauty, its amiable charm.

IMAGE 6 FEET, 5 INCHES TALL; BERNICE P. BISHOP MUSEUM, HONOLULU

8

PAINTING BY RICHARD SCHLECHT, BASED ON BATHYMETRIC STUDIES OF BRUCE C. HEEZEN
OF THE LAMONT-DOHERTY GEOLOGICAL OBSERVATORY AND MARIE THARP OF THE U.S. NAVAL OCEANOGRAPHIC OFFICE.

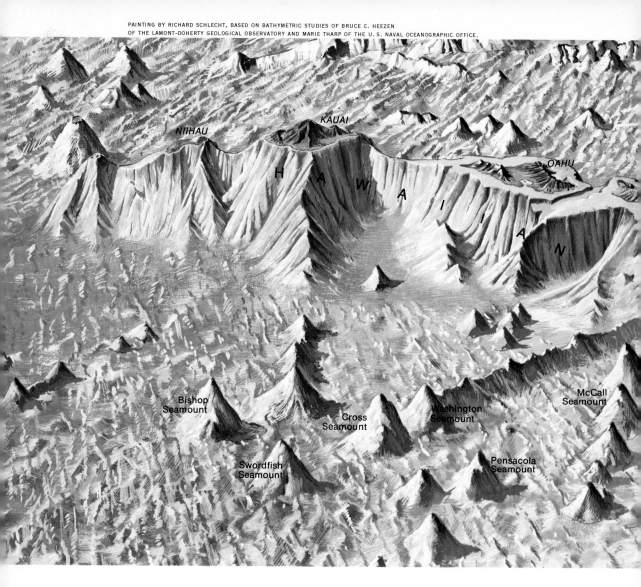

In a Pacific emptied of water, mountains of the Hawaiian Ridge climb from abyssal depths to thrust summits high above sea level. Of the 132 Hawaiian Islands, reaching across 1,600 miles of ocean, only seven—Hawaii, Maui, Molokai, Lanai, Oahu, Kauai, and Niihau—have significant human populations. The ridge's infinitesimally slow birth began 25 million years ago when a fissure in the sea floor started spewing molten rock that formed rough spheres of "pillow lava" like those at right. Divers 160 feet down off the Kona coast of Hawaii glide above this algae-covered formation. Measured from the ocean floor, Mauna Kea on the Island of Hawaii stands as the world's tallest mountain, rising 19,680 feet to sea level and another 13,796 feet to its peak.

MOLOKAI

LANAI

MAUI

KAHOOLAWE

HAWAIIAN

RIDGE

HAWAII

Mauna Kea

HAWAIIAN

DEEP

ARCH

MOLOKAI FRACTURE ZONE

Wini Seamount

Apuupuu Seamount

Richard Schlecht

Polynesian pilgrims—Hawaii's founding fathers—approach their new home-
land in this stylized artist's impression. Some authorities believe they first
stepped ashore on the Island of Kauai. Culmination of the prehistoric migra-
tions that peopled the islands of the Pacific, this landfall occurred about A.D.
750. Double-hulled canoes as long as 80 feet and powered by claw-shaped sails

LEO AND DIANE DILLON

*could carry a hundred people on voyages of thousands of miles. Hawaii's set-
tlers, many archeologists think, came from the Marquesas Islands, far to the
southeast, on a voyage of exploration. Navigators drew upon extensive knowledge of winds, currents, and heavens. Sugarcane, banana, coconut, and sweet
potato plants survived the journey and thrived, as did dogs, chickens, and pigs.*

Hawaiian high chief Boki (left) governed the Island of Oahu early in the 19th century. A helmet of ieie vine rootlets covered with feathers complements his velvet-soft feather cloak. His wife Liliha wears a badge of rank—a lei of human hair hung with a whale-tooth ornament. Stringent kapus, *or taboos, regulated social and religious behavior; executioners dealt harshly with violators (below). Above, Diamond Head looms beyond islanders fishing and gathering seaweed in the shallows.*

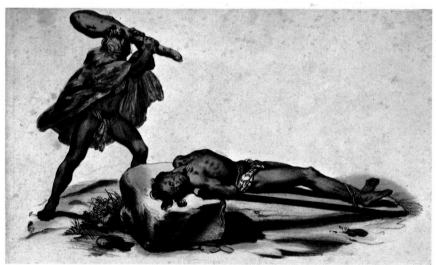

abyssal depths, islands of Hawaii began life some 25,000,000 years ago.

I had learned of the spheres before coming to Hawaii from a friend of Jim's, Dr. James G. Moore of the U. S. Geological Survey at Menlo Park in California. A veteran of many years' underwater research in Hawaii, Dr. Moore had encountered the spheres at extreme depths through the use of dredges and remotely controlled cameras. Later he discovered identical formations in shallower water, diving in company with Jim. He suggested I dive and see them personally if I got the chance.

I hesitated at first. Basalt, after all, is nothing more than lava and Hawaii has plenty of that. I asked what was so special about the spheres.

"The very fact that they're spheres," Dr. Moore had answered. "You won't find lava like that anywhere on land in Hawaii except in some dried-up prehistoric marsh. We call it 'pillow lava,' and it's peculiar to submarine volcanic eruptions. Cold water surrounding the molten flow turns the outer skin to something almost like rubber, so that as more lava boils up from below, the skin stretches to form domes or pillows. After a while the pillows harden and the lava finds other outlets, building more pillows, and still more, in astronomical numbers.

"On land," Dr. Moore added, "lava takes entirely different shapes, such as the taffylike *pahoehoe* and a clinker type known as *aa*. But the surface area of Hawaii represents the mere tips of gigantic sea mountains. We estimate that the major portion of the islands—including their original base—consists of pillow lava. Yet few people have ever seen it in its natural state. Jim Robinson is a charter fisherman and diver at Kailua on the Island of Hawaii, and he knows a formation you can reach with scuba gear. If you're interested in the birth of the islands, go and see him."

Now across the intervening twilight Jim beckons me toward one of the larger spheres, a boulder some five feet in diameter. As I swim over, he scrapes at the surface with his fingers. A faint cloud of gray algae blossoms and drifts away, exposing a patch of smooth stone almost the same lifeless color. Jim points to other boulders alongside and underneath the first one, and I see that all are linked in a single mass, like some huge pile of cannonballs welded together at random.

Hawaii's first king—a skilled general and a wise leader—Kamehameha I seized power in the late 18th century.

Jim glances at his watch and spreads the fingers of one hand: At this depth and with single air tanks we can stay only five more minutes. He motions me toward a nearby rise where the boulders seem to have sprouted one on top of another and abruptly ended in a sharp ridgeline.

We reach the crest and I find it is only an illusion. The spheres continue down the opposite slope in a vast and motionless cascade, gradually disappearing in the lavender immensity of depth and time to some remote crucible of origin. It is a spectacular sight, and somehow a chilling one. At Jim's signal I gladly turn and start upward through zones of shadow toward the welcoming world of light.

No one knows who first saw it, that great armada of islands ranged in ragged convoy across 1,600 miles of the mid-Pacific. Very probably the earliest settlers came from the Marquesas Islands about A.D. 750, steering their double-hulled canoes across 2,400 miles of unknown ocean with neither compass nor charts to guide them—a triumph of seamanship unexcelled either by the Vikings or the Phoenicians.

Hawaii was the last of the great ocean frontiers known to have been conquered by the Polynesian people, according to Dr. Kenneth P. Emory, the great authority on Polynesian culture and history at Honolulu's Bernice Pauahi Bishop Museum.

"Their ocean-wide voyaging," he told me when I called on him, "began on the western borders of Polynesia, quite possibly in the Fiji Islands region, about 1500 B.C. It was there that the Polynesians emerged as a group distinct from all other peoples in terms of language, culture, and physical makeup. Doubtless they had common ancestry with other Pacific peoples, reaching back several millenniums to what is now Southeast Asia." He paused, then waved through his office window toward a small garden, lush in the tropical sun.

"As to what drove the Polynesians on their great voyages, I would say that one of the chief forces is right there—good land, and the food it could supply. Over the centuries the Marquesas, like a number of other Pacific island groups, have been plagued by recurring drought. They could never have supported a large population for any length of time; hence they became an early center of dispersal.

"Hawaii, with its ideal climate, its relatively large expanse and variety of land, must have looked like paradise to those early Marquesans—and to others, such as the Tahitians, who followed them."

Not to mention the British, Russians, Americans, French, Chinese, Japanese, Mexicans, Filipinos, and any number of others who came in their turn and to whom Hawaii also looked like paradise. In most cases Hawaii lived up to the image, though now and then paradise proved to be a mirage. Yet few who came to settle ever gave up and returned home. As a result, Hawaiians today are an incredible mixture of nationalities involving literally scores of combinations, with pure Polynesians reduced to less than one percent of the island's 700,000 permanent inhabitants, and Caucasians—or *haoles,* to use the Hawaiian word—accounting for less than 20 percent. Hawaiians of Japanese ancestry are the largest group, with nearly 35 percent of the total.

Feathered image of Kukailimoku, personal war god to King Kamehameha I, bares dogs' teeth in a fierce scowl.

Intermarriage contributes both to the joy of Hawaiians and to the confusion of newcomers, for there are Joneses and Baileys in Hawaii today with as much Oriental blood in their veins as in those of the Lins, the Chus, and the Sakamuras. Such a mixture helps to explain Hawaii's climate of tolerance and comparative lack of racial problems. As a Hawaiian friend recently remarked to me, "How can you have discrimination in a place where everybody's a member of a minority group?"

The answer, of course, is that you still can, and Hawaii does, but it is nonetheless well named the Aloha State. During three months of travel throughout the major islands and many of the smaller ones, I heard that familiar Hawaiian word of both greeting and farewell, "Aloha," hundreds of times, yet never without the ring of real warmth.

Behind the smile and the aloha, however, there are many Hawaiis— some of them little-known to mainland Americans.

First of all, there is the Hawaii of pure geography, a great elongated strand of 132 islands, shoals, pinnacles, and reefs with a combined area of 6,450 square miles, roughly equal to that of Connecticut and Rhode

Frenzied fighting topples defeated warriors from a precipice during the Battle of Nuuanu Pali, last major engagement fought by Kamehameha I in his drive to subjugate the islands. In this impressionistic and poetic version of the action, the chief of the Island of Hawaii, leading a force of some 16,000, defeats Chief

LEO AND DIANE DILLON

Kalanikupule of Oahu in April of 1795. Some defenders, preferring death to capture, leaped from the towering cliff. Legend says Kalanikupule escaped and wandered for weeks in the mountains before his capture and sacrificial execution. In 1810, with all resistance crushed, Kamehameha consolidated his kingdom.

Island. Of the islands only seven are inhabited to any real degree—Hawaii, the largest, Maui, Molokai, Lanai, Oahu, Kauai, and Niihau.

Through a curious holdover from an ancient Hawaiian land division, Honolulu, the state capital, is the world's longest city, stretching 1,367 miles southeast to northwest, encompassing a dozen islands and lying across two time zones. The tiny atoll of Kure, on the far northwestern tip of the Honolulu District, is actually closer to the distant Marshall Islands than to what officially is the other side of town!

Hawaii, not Florida, has the southernmost point of land in the United States—Ka Lae, or South Cape, on the Island of Hawaii. Geologically, the same island is the fastest-growing part of the United States, thanks to two active volcanoes, Mauna Loa and Kilauea, which occasionally add enormous quantities of lava to the island's area and mass.

In addition, the State of Hawaii is the fastest-moving one of the 50—the islands as a whole creep steadily toward Japan by some four inches a year, several times the rate of the North American continental drift.

Finally, Hawaii has what is technically the world's tallest mountain, Mauna Kea on the Island of Hawaii. From its base on the ocean floor it rises 19,680 feet to sea level, and another 13,796 feet to its frequently snow-covered summit—a total of 33,476 feet. By comparison, Mount Everest in the Himalayas reaches a mere 29,028 feet.

The wonder is that the Spaniards missed the archipelago for more than two centuries, during the age of the great galleon voyages from Manila to Mexico's west coast. Yet Hawaii somehow eluded European navigators until January 18, 1778, when England's brilliant explorer, Capt. James Cook, sighted the Island of Oahu. Two days later he landed at Kauai, Oahu's neighbor to the northwest. Within little more than a year, on his second visit to the islands, Cook lost his life in a skirmish with natives at Kealakekua Bay on the Island of Hawaii.

Cook called his discovery the Sandwich Islands, after one of his patrons, the Earl of Sandwich. Happily for everyone, the name gradually gave way to the ancient Polynesian term, *Hawai'i,* whose exact meaning, despite countless claims, no one really knows. Such was their love for the verdant islands that in their ancient poetry the Polynesians called them *Hawai'i kua uli*—"green-backed Hawaii."

Others since then have been equally enraptured. Mark Twain called Hawaii "the loveliest fleet of islands that lies anchored in any ocean," and he declared that "no other land could so longingly and so beseechingly haunt me, sleeping and waking." Jack London fell in love with Hawaii, declaring, "The older I grow, the oftener I come back...." For simple eloquence, however, few have matched the words of Charles A. Lindbergh, who has done much to help preserve Hawaii's natural beauty. Visualizing the islands in a vast setting of night, Lindbergh wrote that they "appear held up by water and pressed down by stars."

There are times when Hawaii, or at least Oahu, appears pressed down by the sheer weight of human bodies, in the form of some 1,400,000 annual tourists. Nor is Mark Twain's fleet of beloved islands apt to lighten ship in the near future: Forecasts run as high as 3,000,000 tourists a year by 1978—more than four times the islands' current population.

PAINTING BY GEORGE CARTER, C. 1783, BERNICE P. BISHOP MUSEUM

*"One of the Chiefs more daring than the rest steep'd behind and stab'd him betwixt
the sholders with an Iron Dagger. . . ." Thus Captain Cook died on the Island
of Hawaii in 1779 at the hands of the people he discovered. A crew member
described the tragedy, a senseless skirmish over a stolen cutter. The Sandwich
Islands, as Cook named them for an English patron, soon became a trading cross-
roads, with whalers and fur traders anchoring regularly to replenish provisions.*

Calvinist missionaries confront aboriginal Hawaiians at Honolulu on April 17, 1820. Drawn to the islands by reports of wickedness and the Biblical mandate "Go ye into all the world and preach...," the stern New Englanders built churches and schools, taught the islanders to read and write, translated

LEO AND DIANE DILLON

the Bible, ministered to the sick, and studied the melodious language of the islands. Charged with bringing the Hawaiians "to the mansions of eternal blessedness," the missionaries strove to convey to them the unfamiliar abstractions of Christianity; in the first 17 years they accepted only about 1,300 converts.

For the moment tourism ranks second to United States military spending in Hawaii's list of financial assets. The great bases such as Pearl Harbor Naval Station, Hickam Air Force Base, Schofield Barracks, and the Kaneohe Bay Marine Corps Air Station—all of them on Oahu—help to provide Hawaii with a yearly defense income of some $606,000,000, and a military population of more than 100,000, including dependents. War in Viet Nam has brought a flow of 197,000 servicemen a year on "R & R"—rest and recuperation—for individual periods of a week, with the addition of a matching number of loved ones from the mainland.

Gradually tourism is overtaking the military as Hawaii's chief source of income, providing a total in 1968 of $460,000,000. Those two familiar symbols of the islands, sugarcane and pineapple, trailed far behind with $201,000,000 and $127,600,000 respectively.

So much for statistics; they provide no more than a bare outline of Hawaii. Color and variety stem from other aspects of island life, such as that wondrous example of spoken music, the Hawaiian language. Few except scholars and those of Polynesian origin speak it fluently, for the language of most islanders today is more than 99 percent English. The remaining fraction of a percent, however, is pure Hawaiian, and essential to everyday life. Even the rawest newcomer quickly learns a handful of words, including the one for himself—*malihini,* stranger.

The early Hawaiians were strangers themselves to the written word, having managed for centuries with an assortment of crude symbols and pictographs. It fell to the first American missionaries to Hawaii in the 1820's to transform into script what sounds more than anything else like a mountain stream bubbling over polished stones.

The missionaries accomplished the job with only 12 letters—seven consonants and five fearfully overworked vowels—in combinations as melodious and unmanageable as any in the history of human expression.

Take, for example, *Hamakuaikapaiaalaikahala*—a type of hold in the ancient Hawaiian art of *lua,* or hand-to-hand combat.

"Hamakua," an authority on the sport explained to me, "is a former district on the Island of Maui. Literally, Hamakuaikapaiaalaikahala means 'Hamakua of the bowers fragrant with pandanus'—a not uncommon example of Hawaiian poetic speech." He grinned.

"In fact, it takes a good lua wrestler almost as much time to pronounce the hold as it does to apply it!"

When it comes to personal names, the Hawaiian language takes off in an uncontrolled rhapsody of poetic composition. A good friend of mine, a charming woman on the Island of Kauai, goes by the first name of Maile. I once asked her what it meant.

"It's a type of flowering vine with aromatic leaves," she answered, "but of course that's only my nickname. The real one"—she took a breath—"is Mailelauliilii Hoapilimakaieie. It means 'The small, fragrant maile vine closely entwined with the climbing ieie plant of the upland forests.'"

As it happens, Maile's last name is more of a problem for her fellow Hawaiians to pronounce than her first one. She married an American of Yugoslav descent, another good friend of mine, Bob Semitekol. "Semitekol," says Bob cheerfully, "doesn't mean a thing."

Leader in 1820 of the first missionaries to Hawaii, Hiram Bingham sat with his wife Sybil for this portrait by artist-inventor Samuel F. B. Morse in 1819.

Fortunately, most of the pure Hawaiian words in common use throughout the islands are as short and simple as their English counterparts. Hawaiians of every national strain say *pau* (POW) for finished, *puka* (poo-ka) for a hole, *keiki* (kay-kee) for a baby or child, and *wahine* (wa-HEE-neh) for a wife or woman. Of the two words for man — *kane* (KA-neh) and *kanaka* (kah-NAH-kah) — the latter can convey either great affection or disrespect, depending on the speaker's tone.

For descendants of mariners, Hawaiians have curious gaps in their language — for example, there is no real word for "weather." As for direction, the islanders prefer to relate to things close at hand rather than to abstract points of the compass. Two prime examples are the universally used words, *mauka* and *makai,* the former meaning "toward the mountains" and the latter "toward the sea."

Occasionally landmarks serve in place of directions, as in the case of Ewa and Diamond Head on the Island of Oahu. Ewa is a plantation area to the west of Honolulu, and Diamond Head, of course, is the famous volcanic peak east of the city. Honolulu residents use the two place-names to indicate west and east respectively. To newcomers unfamiliar with the custom but having a smattering of island geography, it is disconcerting to hear a football broadcaster at a high-school game announce, "Punahou kicks off, and it's a high one, Ewa-Diamond Head" — seemingly a kick of some 15 miles.

At least one gap in the Hawaiian language reflects the islanders' instinctive generosity. Although there is a much-used word for "Thank you" — *Mahalo* — there is no real equivalent of "You're welcome." The sentiment is taken for granted.

Hawaii's official motto conveys the same sense of basic gentleness and decency among her people. Composed in 1843 by King Kamehameha III, it declares: *Ua Mau Ke Ea O Ka Aina I Ka Pono* — "The life of the land is perpetuated in righteousness."

After Kamehameha's time Hawaii passed from the status of kingdom to republic in 1894, to United States Territory in 1900, and finally to 50th State in 1959, not always with righteousness and certainly not always in peace. But the life of the land has been preserved by a Hawaiian spirit that has survived triumph and tragedy for more than 1,200 years.

For an over-all view of the Hawaiian islands, nothing can quite match a personal tour with my friend Charles R. (Bud) Whitman. At the time of my visit Bud was a captain in the U. S. Air Force and a flight instructor with a squadron of T-33 jets at Hickam Air Force Base just west of Honolulu. One afternoon I sat buckled in the rear seat of a T-33 while Bud rolled us down the huge runway Hickam shares with Honolulu International Airport and lifted the nose into a clear Pacific sky.

I had asked Bud to show me as many of the major islands as he could, together with any features that were particular favorites of his. We skimmed eastward — or rather, Diamond Head — along Honolulu's heavily developed waterfront, past an expanse of high-rise hotels with a narrow threshold of sand that marks the city's world-famous Waikiki Beach. Behind the huge glass-and-concrete columns Honolulu stretched white and gleaming toward the mountain slopes, like some gigantic wave

Wooden dolls made by Bingham for his daughters Lydia and Sophia, born in Hawaii, wear dresses of fine cotton.

cresting a breakwater in cascades of foam. Here, within little more than one percent of Hawaii's area, nearly half of her people are concentrated.

Beyond Diamond Head, Bud climbed to 12,000 feet and set a course east-southeast for the Island of Hawaii, largest and geologically youngest in the chain. Over the intercom he identified various other islands as they slipped beneath us, adding details about their makeup and history.

The first was Molokai, set like a green shoe on the blue carpet of the Pacific with the toe pointing due east. To the south lay the smaller islands of Lanai and Kahoolawe, the one a center of pineapple production and the other an uninhabited Navy and Marine Corps target range. Still farther to the east lay the great hourglass shape of the Island of Maui.

"They're all youngsters compared to most of the chain," Bud said, "with an age as actual islands of about one to two million years. Some of the older ones to the northwest of Oahu may have poked their heads above the surface as far back as 10 million years, though of course it took them something like 25 million years to reach that level from the ocean floor. There's the baby of the group," he added, tilting the nose down so that I could see the silhouettes of two massive cones blotting out the horizon ahead and to the southeast.

"That's Hawaii, with Mauna Kea on the left and Mauna Loa to the right. It's still about 90 miles away, so you can get an idea of why Hawaiians call it the 'Big Island'—it's larger than all the other 131 put together. As an island, it's probably less than half a million years old, and it's still going strong. Mauna Loa erupted the last time in 1950, and Kilauea on the other side of it seems to be in action half the time these days. It's a little far to the Big Island with our fuel supply, so I'll show you another crater close up. They call it Haleakala—roughly, 'house of the sun.' "

Letting down to 7,000 feet, Bud swung toward the Island of Maui, approaching it from the north and flying between two volcanic masses across a low isthmus that gives Maui its nickname, the "Valley Island."

Once through the divide he climbed sharply to the left and we suddenly crested the rim of the most enormous crater I have ever seen. It stretched beneath us for miles like some vast open-hearth furnace shut down moments before. Repeated eruptions had tempered and scorched the walls and floor of the basin to deep red, streaked with life-less grays and blacks. Far below, the surface was studded with the dark pinnacles and eroded cones that had fired the monstrous caldron.

"It's dormant now," Bud said reassuringly and then added, not so reassuringly, "it blew up the last time from one of its flanks in 1790. The guidebooks say it's the largest crater in the world, but it isn't—just one of the largest. Still, it's 21 miles around the rim and one and a half times the size of Manhattan. Let's have a look inside."

With that, Bud tilted over and we streaked down one side of the crater, beginning a circuit of the western end several hundred feet above the floor and balancing more or less on one wing tip. Twenty-one miles

Kamehameha I, memorialized in bronze in downtown Honolulu, extends an upturned palm in welcome—the gesture of aloha. Some 1,400,000 tourists annually spend more than $450,000,000 viewing the old king's realm.

NATIONAL GEOGRAPHIC PHOTOGRAPHER BATES LITTLEHALES

suddenly shrank to nothing, and I found myself plastered to the seat as though I were riding a giant centrifuge. But the view made up for it, as we gazed down the dead throats of cones and at the endlessly varied shapes of the lava spires. Then we were up and out of the crater through a great breach in the wall forced by some ancient lava flow.

From Haleakala we turned northwest toward Oahu again, making a low-level pass across the sheer cliffs at the eastern end of Molokai and skirting a broad, almost inaccessible tongue of land with a small village known as Kalaupapa, a Hawaiian term meaning "flat reef." The name gives no hint of the peninsula's dark history as a place of exile for Hawaii's lepers during more than a century. In the distance I made out the shape of a small airstrip along the edge of the peninsula and noted down Kalaupapa as a place to visit on a future tour of Molokai.

Bud had saved enough fuel to take in the last two major islands of the chain, Kauai and Niihau, some 70 miles northwest of Oahu.

"They call Kauai the 'Garden Island,'" Bud said, "and you'll see why in a few minutes. Even to Hawaiians, who tend to take tropical paradises for granted, Kauai is something special. Like most of the other islands it has a wet and a dry side—windward and leeward—caused by the trade winds' dumping their rain on the northeastern slopes of the mountains and having nothing left for the other side. One of the highest peaks, Waialeale, has had as much as 52 *feet* of rain in a single year, making it the wettest spot on earth. Yet a mile or so down the leeward slope of the same mountain it's practically desert."

We approached Kauai on its wet side, an immense, luxuriant shield to the wind. It made me think of a line by historian J. C. Beaglehole in his description of the discovery of another Pacific paradise, Tahiti—"Green stood up that island in the sea. . . ."

Kauai that day stood blossoming as well as green. Viewed from low level the scalloped coast wore a bright hem of flowering trees and shrubs, combining the reds and yellows of hibiscus with the pinks and whites of plumeria, the violet of jacaranda, and the scarlet of bougainvillea and poinciana. In the dense green mat of upland forest beyond, a scattering of African tulip trees winked bright orange. Still higher, the mountains disappeared in a heavy layer of cloud packed around the heights by the trade winds.

South and west of Lihue, Kauai's county seat, the land evened out in a coarse embroidery of sugarcane with random villages worked into the design. As we approached the island's leeward side I noticed a gradual change in the color of the ocean beneath us. Normally Hawaii's waters display varying shades of indigo, violet, and turquoise that shift according to the depth. Now the change was to dull brown, then tan, and finally almost to red. I mentioned it to Bud.

"That's Waimea Canyon at work," he said, pointing to a gap in the line of mountains rising several miles inland. "It's sort of a giant drainage ditch for Waialeale. On the mountain's leeward side there's almost no vegetation to hold the soil when the water comes streaming down from the top, so a lot of red volcanic mud washes into the sea. That's how the area gets its name, Waimea, meaning 'reddish water.' When you come

Adrift in a sea of luggage, arriving tourists cluster at Honolulu International Airport. Outside, a vendor fashions a lei of croton leaves. Ancient Polynesians, lacking gems and gold, strung island flowers into leis and presented them as tokens of esteem; today the garlands symbolize Hawaiian hospitality.

Proud progeny of a mid-Pacific melting pot, Hawaiian Islanders exhibit characteristics bestowed by diverse ancestry. Skin colors range from delicate pink to copper. Straight black hair predominates. Beginning in 1852, planters imported some 46,000 Chinese to work the sugar plantations. In the 1880's, Japanese and Portuguese arrived. During the 20th century, about 125,000 Filipino laborers have settled on the plantations, along with Koreans, Spaniards, and Puerto Ricans. Mixture of the races and nationalities has increased. Half a century ago 12 percent of the marriages in Hawaii were interracial. World War I hurried the trend and now about a third are. Pure Hawaiians may soon disappear entirely. From a high of 300,000 when Captain Cook landed, their numbers have shrunk to fewer than 7,000. Today's islanders represent a rich blend of Yankee ingenuity, Oriental industry, and native good will; each element sparkles with uniqueness in a broad mosaic of Hawaiian culture remarkably free of racial tension and strife.

N.G.S. PHOTOGRAPHERS JAMES L. AMOS (TOP ROW: 2ND FROM LEFT; MIDDLE ROW: 1ST AND 3RD; BOTTOM ROW: 2ND AND 3RD) AND BATES LITTLEHALES

back to Kauai, go and have a look at where that soil comes from. You'll think you're standing right on the very rim of the Grand Canyon."

On our seaward side and at some 10 miles' distance another island appeared, its long, tapering silhouette reminiscent of a sperm whale.

"Take a good look," Bud advised. "This is probably as close as you're going to get, although it's true you can fly over it if you want. It's named Niihau, but it's often called the 'Forbidden Island.' About 250 Hawaiians, mostly of pure blood, live on it as cattle and sheep ranchers. The island belongs lock, stock, and barrel to the Robinson family on Kauai, and outsiders are strictly *kapu* —forbidden. The idea seems to be to protect at least one traditional Hawaiian community from being overrun and destroyed by the modern world."

As it turned out, I did get a close, if brief, look at Niihau many weeks later under circumstances involving a helicopter, another memorable pilot, a flock of wild birds, and a cow in desperate trouble. At the time with Bud, however, I took another look, jotted down "Niihau—kapu," and turned to the view close at hand—Kauai's Na Pali Coast.

Both our fuel and the afternoon sun were dwindling, and Bud made a pass along the great rampart, a bluff hundreds of feet high that plunges vertically into the restless sea, with only a tiny crescent of beach here and there to suggest a landing point.

"It's not exactly the spot I'd pick to come ashore even in a flat calm," Bud said, "but some historians think that's just where the first Polynesian arrivals in Hawaii set foot. If you'd been at sea for weeks without sight of land I guess anything would look good, and certainly they were sailors enough to manage it."

Then we were heading for Oahu and home. Beyond Kauai to the far northwest lay a score of smaller islands of the 50th State, a few inhabited, that I would have to see some other way. But the flight had given me an excellent view of the heart of the great galaxy that is Hawaii.

Several miles off Oahu's Kaena Point, Bud picked up Honolulu approach control on the radio, and we began our descent. Along the narrow valleys back of the coast where shadows come early, scattered lights of houses were beginning to wink on. Soon they would filter down across Honolulu itself, until the city became a great floodplain of light washing mauka-makai —from the mountains to the sea.

A mile ahead of us in the approach pattern a four-engine transpacific jet landed and swung smoothly from the runway toward the main terminal. As Bud and I followed suit and began taxiing toward Hickam, another huge jet touched down behind us.

The procession seemed endless. Many aboard the big planes undoubtedly were businessmen with work to do in Honolulu, and other passengers were en route across the Pacific to Australia or the Far East. But a good many more were taking Hawaii at its word, expressed in one of the simplest of island sayings, *E kipa mai* —"Come, enjoy hospitality."

"Unimaginably beautiful," Mark Twain remembered Hawaii, 18 years after his visit. He toured the islands in 1866 as a newspaper correspondent. A vista unchanged since his day: gentle surf washing Sunset Beach on Oahu.

NATIONAL GEOGRAPHIC PHOTOGRAPHER EMORY KRISTOF

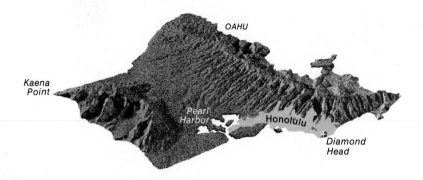

OAHU

Kaena
Point

Pearl
Harbor

Honolulu

Diamond
Head

HONOLULU

High-rise capital of an island paradise

I NEVER learned her last name, but it doesn't matter. She is "Kaimi" to everyone who drops by. In an average week she arranges to welcome several hundred visitors to Honolulu without ever seeing them — Kaimi's customers take care of that part of the job themselves.

I met her one morning at her stall near the entrance to Honolulu's airport, surrounded by a day's work in carnations, plumeria, bougainvillea, vanda orchids, and a bushel or two of yellow ginger. Behind an almost visible cloud of fragrance she was stringing blossoms and leaves into familiar Hawaiian garlands called leis with the lightning skill of a Chinese shopkeeper at his abacus. In a row of neighboring stalls a dozen or more women were doing the same thing. The finished leis hung in a dazzling block-long frieze from the ceilings of the stalls, for sale to anyone meeting an arriving plane or seeing one off.

As it happened I was on my way to meet a typewriter at the air-freight terminal, but I stopped by Kaimi's stall to admire her handiwork. She gave me a smile and a cordial "Aloha"; as we talked, her fingers maintained their rhythmic blur. *(Continued on page 40)*

Beneath a leafy banyan bower at the zoo in Kapiolani Park, the Honolulu Symphony, founded in 1900, plays a Saturday concert. Honolulans revel in the happy blend of arts and tropical out-of-doors their lively city offers year-round.

Overleaf: *Like a great wave, the city of Honolulu curls about Diamond Head crater (lower right), crests just below Punchbowl crater (lower left), and surges up slopes of the Koolau Range. Port, tourist playground, military base—these functions help mix nationalities and push the city's hectic growth. This area of Oahu's south coast teems with almost half the state's people.*

DONALD J. CRUMP, NATIONAL GEOGRAPHIC STAFF (BELOW), AND N.G.S. PHOTOGRAPHER JAMES L. AMOS

Surfside parade: Waikiki Beach shimmers with bright colors and burnished bodies. In front of the Royal Hawaiian Hotel trade winds ripple the palms. Visitors by the thousand—85 percent of Hawaii's tourists—converge on the famous strip. All come for the action: Many watch, some bask, some paddle the hotel's 30-foot outrigger. The boldest rent surfboards (far left) to try their luck with the long green swells. At day's end, a surfer meets friends ashore (left).

From Kaimi I learned several things about flowers in Hawaii, including the fact that the hibiscus, not the orchid, is the official state blossom. Both kinds of flowers come in a wide selection; orchids alone run to more than 20,000 varieties in the islands, counting both the wild and the constantly increasing hybrid strains. Commonest among them all is the miniature vanda joachim, the type Kaimi had, a rather perishable crimson, purple, and white orchid that ends up in everything throughout Hawaii from leis and buttonholes to steak platters at exclusive restaurants.

During some 15 minutes Kaimi dispatched half a dozen leis to hurried customers, several of them old friends, for prices ranging from two dollars to seven. I began to feel in the way since I wasn't a customer, and I said my alohas to Kaimi. She reached into a basket behind her and produced a small white orchid of a kind I hadn't seen before, tucked it in my lapel, and waved me away as I reached for my wallet.

"Nobody," she explained smiling, "should leave without something."

Kaimi's remark, in quite a different sense, is echoed by more than one tourist as he departs from Honolulu after a vacation. The tourist is referring to the state of his finances and Honolulu's ability to deplete them. The complaint is an old one and it has some justification: Hawaii, especially Honolulu, has one of the highest costs of living in the United States—roughly 20 percent above the national average.

What grieves the people of Hawaii is that the tourist has a good deal to do with the fact, yet for him the burden is only temporary; if the pinch gets too tight he can always leave. But for an islander high prices are an inescapable fact of life. If Hawaiians have one of the highest average family incomes among the 50 states, they also have the greatest percentage of working wives—the only way some families can make ends meet.

"In some respects Honolulu is a bargain-basement city," says Robert C. Schmitt, Hawaii's brilliant and personable State Statistician. For a short course in Hawaiian economics I had called on Bob one morning at his office in Honolulu's spectacular new State Capitol, near the former royal residence known as Iolani Palace.

"Mostly, the bargains have to do with climate," Bob explained. "Like many other parts of Hawaii, Honolulu varies in temperature no more than a few degrees on either side of 75° F. As a result we have almost no heating bills and we can go a little light on clothes. But Hawaii isn't really an industrial state, and it's far removed from the states that are. To start with, we're 2,397 miles from San Francisco, and that means quite a freight bill on mainland goods. Add a tourist-oriented economy to the equation, and Hawaii has a few statistics she could do without.

"For example," Bob continued, "food costs us 18 percent more than it does the rest of the country, and housing costs up to a whopping 41 percent more in some categories. Land prices are so high that most people would rather lease a lot than buy it—that way they can afford to build a house. Even so, on a percentage basis fewer residents of Hawaii own their own homes than the people of any other state."

As a portrait of paradise, it sounded a bit grim. Bob shook his head.

"You don't see us leaving in droves," he said. "In fact, it's the other way around. Metropolitan Honolulu, which takes in all of Oahu, still ranks

Prospector Lillian Risk scours Waikiki with a metal detector. Pinging earphones direct her to stop and sift. Her pastime trove: keys, coins, bottle caps, and jewels.

among the 10 fastest-growing major cities in the U. S., with an increase in population of 29 percent over the last decade. The total now stands at 645,000. Besides that, we've got at least two things no paradise should be without—youth and beauty. Hawaiians are the youngest people of any state, with a median age of 24.3 years. As for beauty," he added, grinning, "our women seem to rate pretty high with their men—Hawaii has more florists per capita than any other state in the Union! If you want to argue the point, that figure is exactly 20.8 florists for every 100,000 Hawaiians."

Who wants to argue? Hawaii's women are unquestionably beautiful, a fact that adds a great deal to the charm of Honolulu. Not that the city needs all that much help, according to Mike Hoomanawanui. I rode with Mike for an afternoon aboard his sightseeing bus, one of hundreds in Honolulu that contribute daily to the enlightenment of tourists and to the paralysis of city traffic.

Mike is both guide and driver on the bus, and Honolulu traffic jams don't trouble him at all. As he explained to my fellow sightseers and me, his last name, Hoomanawanui, is Hawaii's unofficial motto.

"In island language," he announced, "*hoomanawanui* means—'Take it easy, don't be in a hurry; today is so beautiful, why reach for tomorrow?'"

Or as the dictionary puts it, with none of Mike's gift for poetic expression, "hoomanawanui . . . patience."

With the exercise of a little hoomanawanui and with Mike's knowledge of Honolulu we saw a good bit of his hometown, beginning with that feature of virtually every island tour, Waikiki Beach.

Actually, Waikiki is no different from a score of other resort beaches in Hawaii except in the size and glitter of its hotels and office buildings, driven like an immense row of ornate pilings into a strip of Honolulu's waterfront. Behind the barricade, along Waikiki's Kalakaua Avenue, flows a human tide as varied and iridescent as Hawaii's waters. The sidewalks were awash with tourists in blindingly colorful aloha shirts and muumuus—the graceful ankle-length island dresses—interspersed with equally blinding young girls in bikinis and the inevitable surfers in ragged shorts, maneuvering their fiberglass boards through the crowds with the same effortless skill they show on the water.

Pedestrians and motorists were bombarded on all sides by the sounds of Waikiki—loudspeakers blaring an incredible assortment of rock and Hawaiian love songs from restaurants and cafes, the shrill of police whistles, the bleat of horns, and the thunderous chime of pile driver against steel as Waikiki builds itself ever newer and larger.

"Some people complain that it's artificial," Mike said with a wave at the scene, "and in at least one sense there's no argument: Waikiki used to be mostly swamp until the city drained and filled it. The name means 'spouting water,' probably from springs in the swamp."

Farther along Kalakaua Avenue the buildings gave way to open beach, with a panorama of swimmers and sunbathers burnished varying shades of mahogany. Beyond stretched the luminous green expanse of sea, streaked in endlessly dissolving patterns by the white wakes of surfers.

From Waikiki, Mike turned inland toward everyday Honolulu, where the metropolis soon sheds its boardwalk atmosphere and becomes an

average American city — with exceptions. Among clusters of school children drifting back to afternoon classes I noticed a marked scarcity of blond heads and Caucasian faces. Most features were Polynesian and Oriental or a soft blend of the two, under uniformly lustrous black hair.

Honolulu's neighborhoods reveal a matching blend of cultures, faiths, and customs. Within the space of a block or so I counted two Protestant churches, a Buddhist temple, a Singapore bank, two hamburger stands, a Japanese teahouse, and a pizza parlor.

Even in the field of sports Honolulu happily combines elements of both East and West. Newcomers to the municipal stadium are startled to find their fellow baseball fans clamoring for the umpire's scalp in faultless Brooklynese, while devouring gingery *teriyaki* steaks and *saimin,* a kind of Oriental noodle soup.

Later I was to find that other time-honored American institutions cheerfully bow to island tastes. At its store in Honolulu's gigantic Ala Moana Center, Sears, Roebuck and Co. serves poi to employees and their guests in the cafeteria. Mainlanders normally pass the offering by, complaining that the traditional Hawaiian dish made of boiled and ground taro root mixed with water is a soggy creation lacking almost all taste. Displaying typical courtesy, Hawaiians refrain from pointing out that the same description could apply to a mainland favorite, mashed potatoes.

With the ease of long practice Mike guided us through a number of stops, leading off with Iolani ("Bird of Heaven") Palace. Here the Hawaiian monarchy ended its faltering days in 1893 under ruthless pressure

Tide of tourist dollars — second only to military revenues — rises with a new hotel below Diamond Head. Transforming Waikiki's skyline, high-rise buildings sprout along Kalakaua Avenue (below), bright showcase for Hawaii's goods. Despite high pay, workers like the one at left find living expensive.

NATIONAL GEOGRAPHIC PHOTOGRAPHERS JAMES L. AMOS (BOTTOM) AND BATES LITTLEHALES

Pursuit of excellence — with Hawaiian flavor — absorbs students at The Kamehameha Schools. Whether churning the pool on their 618-acre campus or painting on the second-grade floor, youngsters follow the 1884 behest of founder Bernice Pauahi Bishop, great-granddaughter of Kamehameha I, to become "good and industrious." The school enrolls some 2,500 children of Hawaiian ancestry.

Youth and a purely American joy in the crunch of football shine from faces at the Honolulu Stadium. Punahou School players in white jerseys tangle with the maroon line of Farrington High. More than 22,000 fans jammed the stands for this Thanksgiving Day doubleheader. With only one university in the far-flung islands, spectators turn enthusiastically to high-school ball. Such is the mania that watchers rise early to see mainland games on TV relayed by satellite. Jets bring television tapes of other games for rebroadcast.

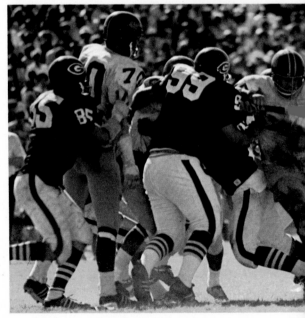

from a group of prominent haoles, who seized control of the government.

"It was pretty direct pressure," Mike remarked as we toured the ornate, musty throne room bordered by an old-fashioned stone veranda. "They simply imprisoned the queen, Liliuokalani, as a threat to stable government and in 1894 declared Hawaii a republic.

"Liliuokalani did much better as a musician than as a stateswoman," he added. "She composed a number of beautiful songs, including the famous 'Aloha Oe,' whose title can mean 'Greetings,' or in this case, 'Farewell to Thee.' After a while they freed Liliuokalani, but it was aloha and farewell to the Hawaiian kingdom."

Back in the bus we had a quick glimpse of the new $30,000,000 State Capitol, vaguely suggestive of a soaring volcano, which houses Hawaii's bicameral legislature.

Beyond the Capitol we skirted the edge of Honolulu's so-called downtown area—not Waikiki, but the financial district adjoining the city's once well-defined Chinatown—and had a view of Kewalo Basin, home to both sport and commercial fishermen.

"With all that water," Mike said, "you'd think Hawaii would be a great commercial fishing center, but it isn't. Believe it or not, our commercial catch is only about one-sixteenth as big as Florida's—roughly 13 million pounds a year. Part of that's due to outdated methods and gear, but there's an invisible reason, too. The Hawaiian Islands are sea mountains, and they don't have the continental shelf that gives some of the other maritime states their big hauls."

For a finale Mike took us high above the center of the city, atop the almost symmetrical volcanic cone known appropriately as the Punchbowl. Around and below us Honolulu arced 360 degrees, from the hillside communities to Tantalus Mountain at our backs, westward toward the vast enclave of Pearl Harbor and along the entire waterfront to the ragged silhouette of Diamond Head crater on the eastern horizon. In the immense grid of avenues and cross streets Mike pointed out a patch or two of green, one of them marking the site of the University of Hawaii and the renowned East-West Center, dedicated to knowledge and understanding throughout the Pacific area.

Certainly the Pacific could use more of both, as the Punchbowl bears silent witness. The great dormant crater is known officially as the National Memorial Cemetery of the Pacific. Here beneath simple flagstone-style markers set in a wide field of grass lie nearly 20,000 dead of World War II, the Korean War, and the Viet Nam conflict. Not all the monuments memorialize Hawaiians, for during World War II many mainland families chose to leave their dead where they had found a last measure of warmth and affection far from home.

Other markers reflect Hawaii's own contribution to a war half a world away. Many inscriptions bear the numerals "442," familiar to all Hawaiians. The numbers stand for the 442nd Regimental Combat Team, the much-decorated unit of second-generation Japanese from Hawaii—all volunteers—who fought brilliantly in Europe during World War II.

As befits a Hawaiian memorial, no race or national group lies separate in the Punchbowl. Walking among the stones, I came across series

of names such as Maeda, Lindner, Kawakami, Cooley, Galase, Dillingham, LeBlanc, and Bordino.

Other names are being added in grim testimony to the fact that the Pacific's troubles are far from over. On our drive back along the rim of the crater the silence was interrupted by the rhythmic crack of three volleys from a rifle squad, followed by the mournful epilogue of Taps.

Later, as we said goodbye, I asked Mike if the Punchbowl had a Hawaiian name, and he nodded.

"They call it *Puowaina*," he answered, "after the pagan ceremonies conducted there long ago by the Polynesian priests. It was never a happy place, that crater. Roughly translated, Puowaina means 'Hill of Sacrifice.' "

Fortunately, Honolulu has other connections with war, such as the job of restoring the morale of those who wage it. One day I waited with some 125 anxious young women at the U.S. Army's Fort De Russy Maluhia Service Club near Waikiki for a flight of servicemen returning on a week's "R & R" from Viet Nam. The period of rest and recuperation is available to military personnel who have served three months or more in the combat zone. Their wives and sweethearts may fly out from the mainland to share it with them.

For what obviously was a happy occasion, I found the atmosphere at Fort De Russy unsettling. Despite the Army's thoughtfulness and planning, the final hour of waiting began to border on the hysterical. Then along came Chaplain Geary.

Wesley V. Geary is a giant of a man, a much-decorated Negro major in the United States Army's Corps of Chaplains, and a great loss to the entertainment world. With a sure instinct for his audience he proceeded to reduce the 125 nervous women to helpless laughter, and to while away 45 otherwise-unendurable minutes.

I don't remember everything Wes Geary told them, but I recall a good deal of sound advice worked in along with the humor — such as the fact that, in addition to being a paradise, Honolulu ranks among the top 10 cities in the country for theft and burglary. While relating this sobering fact Major Geary smoothly extracted a purse with his foot from a chair beside its preoccupied owner, inspected the wallet, and finally handed everything back in disgust.

"Pictures!" he snorted. "No money, just snapshots of *him*! You girls know what the Army pays a chaplain? When you come down here I expect you all to be ready and able to support the church of your choice." He looked around. "And right now, the only choice you got is me."

On the subject of sunbathing Wes cautioned his listeners against an overdose the first day or two of leave. "That Hawaiian sun's mighty

Waiting for strings, ukuleles pile up in the Kamaka Hawaii factory. Gordon Tanoura holds the mold for the curved koa-wood bodies. Ukuleles came from Portugal, but surfboards were born in the Pacific. Honolulan Dick Brewer (above) shapes a "mini" board of his design. Polyurethane forms the core, redwood the spine. Short boards permit such daring maneuvers as a 360-degree turn.

Overleaf: Firecrackers blaze and gongs clang in Chinatown as the lion dancer brings good fortune for the New Year during the annual Narcissus Festival.

At National Memorial Cemetery of the Pacific the dead lie as they fell in battle—without regard to rank or race. A woman pays respects at one of nearly 20,000 markers that pave Punchbowl crater overlooking Honolulu. Japanese-Americans by the thousand served their Nation in World War II. A guard salutes their colors at a ceremony (below) in honor of the Hawaiian 100th Battalion, 442nd Regiment, whose performance on the battlefields of Europe earned seven unit citations and 18,143 individual decorations, and helped advance the cause of statehood for Hawaii. The guard's emblem: the torch of liberty held high.

strong," he said, "and it can spoil your R & R just as easy as it can make it." There were a number of Negro wives in the group, and I noticed they laughed as hard as the rest when he added, "Just look what it did to me."

As Wes talked, an occasional car drew up to the recreation center entrance. Each time, despite their obvious delight with the chaplain, some of the women's nervousness returned. Wes took a stern attitude.

"Now I *told* you I'd let you know when those airport buses are coming," he said, "and Wes Geary, for one, is going to stand clear of you wild stampeding females when they arrive. But you've got to think of the safety of others. Last week about this time a trash van pulled up here with six young soldiers in fatigues. Well, I couldn't hold my girls. Those poor innocent boys took one look at what was coming and lit out for their lives —they're still AWOL in the hills."

At last word came that the buses were on the way. Wes arranged the women in two long lines, so that their men would walk between and each could claim her own.

"Whatever you catch you can keep," were Wes's final words. "But when it's over, remember we're only open five minutes for exchanges."

Then the men were there, and the only exchanges were the wordless ones of joy and of relief from longing. With an enormous smile Wes surveyed 125 couples oblivious of everything but the miracle that enfolded them, and turned companionably to me.

"Now, brother," he said, "let's find ourselves a cup of coffee. There's another miracle due here in exactly three hours."

It is a curious city, Honolulu, one whose image is blurred by its own variety of features, none of them quite outweighing the rest. There is the scenic beauty of a San Francisco, the transient quality of a Washington, D. C., the seafaring aura of a Boston or Charleston, and the distinctive blend of energy and indolence that is pure New Orleans. Honolulu is all, and yet none of them.

In terms of industry, Hawaii's capital city is still hardly more than a processing plant for those two island specialties, pineapple and sugarcane, that are grown throughout the 50th State. Aside from three pineapple canneries and four sugar mills, Honolulu boasts two cement plants, a concrete-pipe factory, a mill for making steel reinforcing rods, one oil refinery, and assorted dredging and construction firms.

Nor is Honolulu a major center of arts and sciences, although its massive University of Hawaii, with a faculty of 2,600 and an enrollment of 18,500, has a growing reputation in such fields as oceanography, Asian and Pacific studies, geophysical sciences, and tropical agriculture.

The real business of Honolulu, military and tourists aside, remains what it was a century ago—the management of Hawaii's 6,450 square miles of varied land, at profits ranging from modest to astronomical. To a large degree the job rests in the hands of a few major companies, known in Hawaii as the "Big Five"—Castle & Cooke, American Factors (AMFAC), Alexander & Baldwin, Theo. H. Davies, and C. Brewer—with competition from such rising firms as Dillingham Corporation, Henry J. Kaiser Associates, and one giant nonprofit trust known as Bishop Estate.

"Of course, land management takes in a lot of things today," said my

friend Frederick Simpich, Jr., a former vice president of Castle & Cooke and son of the late Frederick Simpich, Sr., an assistant editor of NATIONAL GEOGRAPHIC. Fred is an old Hawaii hand, a highly successful author, and a private consultant on land investment in the islands.

"Most of the Big Five," Fred continued, "got their start during the last century in agriculture, principally sugarcane, with control of sizable tracts of land. As time went on they not only increased their land holdings but also branched out in a variety of other fields. Today, for example, Castle & Cooke is involved in everything from pineapple and sugar to shipping, California community development, and even manufacturing.

"Now," Fred added, smiling, "comes the revolution, with the explosion of tourism and immigration. Since World War II land has increased fantastically in value; people have begun pushing pineapple and sugarcane off the map of Oahu. Which doesn't mean that pineapple and sugarcane are dead—Hawaii still needs a diversified economy. But it does mean a whole new concept of land use and development, with wisdom and good taste, I hope. We haven't got much time left."

Time, in the opinion of many, long ago ran out on Honolulu, and the clock has begun ticking for the other islands. No subject today produces more heated argument in the 50th State than the whole question of development versus conservation.

"In some cases," Hawaii's able young Lieutenant Governor, Thomas P. Gill, told me one day, "the so-called 'development' of our islands has shown all the taste and imagination of strip-mining in West Virginia. Land is the coin of the realm to our people, and many of us are sick of seeing it squandered. So far, in Honolulu, we have lost more battles than we have won. But the tide is turning. People are getting tired of speculators and callous developers. Once a Hawaiian gets really angry, watch out."

Even when he isn't angry but only deeply concerned, the Hawaiian can be impressive. I spent an hour or two one afternoon with Kekoa David Kaapu, a Harvard graduate and native of Oahu whose job, at the age of 32, is to bring a sense of order to Honolulu's patchwork growth and redevelopment. As Honolulu's Deputy Managing Director for Housing and Urban Development, Kekoa—or David, as he was known at Harvard—faces a task that would stagger an army of city planners. He approaches it without illusions, yet with considerable confidence in himself and in Hawaii's future.

"From a strictly residential point of view," David told me, "Honolulu is something of a disaster. Among major U.S. cities we rank sixth in the rate of over-all construction, yet last in providing new family housing. You can see why," he added, pointing through the window toward Waikiki. "With land so expensive, developers go for the quickest return, and of course that means tourist facilities such as hotels and restaurants.

"But even when we've built for ourselves," David said, "we made poor use of the land. The average height of buildings in downtown Honolulu

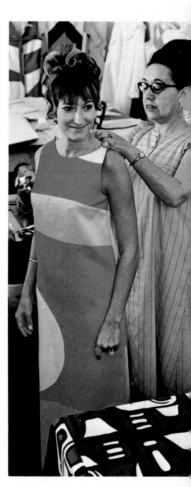

"Aloha" from the drawing board: At Malia Hawaii, Inc., Rogene Radner paints bright patterns for holiday wear. Few can resist such dazzling prints as the one at right; tourists alone spend $55,000,000 annually on fashions.

The world forgotten, Larry and Debbie Connell meet at
Fort De Russy near Waikiki. He flew from duty in Viet
Nam, she from California to share a week of "R & R"
—rest and recuperation—in an armed-forces program
that unites servicemen with their families. Together they
enjoyed a cruise (above). "Mostly," says Debbie, "we
drove around lost most of the time. We had a ball though."
At parting (below), "Larry was very, very comforting."

today is exactly two stories—not what you'd call high-rise. Yet any planner can tell you that the way to open your city up is to concentrate your working and living areas in vertical clusters and put the rest in parks and vistas." He smiled. "It's the old story of 'Stand back and give the victim a little air.' It's a wonder Honolulu's still breathing."

I asked David how he proposed to revive the patient, and he answered seriously, "With an ancient Hawaiian cure, or let's say philosophy. Long ago the island kings granted land to their subjects on the basis of mauka-makai—in narrow tracts stretching inland from the coast to the hilltops. The idea was to follow the natural character of the land, so that a man might enjoy all it had to offer: the pleasures and resources of the sea; the coastal fields; and finally the mountains with their cool heights, their forests, and their views.

"Hawaii's cities of the future should return to the mauka-makai principle," David declared. "Instead of barricading long stretches of coastline, they should reach back from the water's edge naturally, as the land does, beginning low and rising to higher structures in clusters linked by mass transit. That way they would leave broad vistas open to the sea, which belongs not to a lucky few, but to all Hawaiians.

"Yes, I know," he said, anticipating my thought, "Honolulu's built differently, and you can't tear it all down. Imagine trying to dismantle Waikiki! But little by little cities wear out; now's the time to start working on a new one."

Many others in Honolulu today are thinking similar things about distant cities and peoples. On the University of Hawaii's campus, East-West Center students from 44 nations, including the United States, are studying everything from educational psychology to municipal sewage systems for the sake of a better life among their countrymen.

One lunchtime I joined half a dozen students at the cafeteria of the center, whose unwieldy official title is the "Center for Cultural and Technical Interchange Between East and West." All six were in their late 20's or early 30's, most of them graduate students pursuing subjects either unavailable or less advanced in their home countries. Their expenses and tuition came out of some $5,000,000 in federal funds granted each year to the University of Hawaii to run the center.

In a world sorely troubled by racial conflict Honolulu enjoys an image of comparative harmony, despite—or perhaps because of—its multinational character. I asked if the image is a true one.

"On the whole, I think yes," answered Felix Wendt, a tall and likable Western Samoan teacher in his early 30's. "You must remember that Honolulu and the university are not the same thing, but I think people here reflect the city's personality; after all, there are only some 600 of

After 22 months in the fields golden pineapples, some of the crop of 200 million, ride the Dole Company elevator to be washed, peeled, cored, trimmed, sliced, and canned. Strict cleanliness requires constant mending of work gloves (above).

us 'foreign students' in the center, and many thousand Hawaiians at the university. Honolulu's nature seems to me basically tolerant, perhaps a matter of willingness to look beyond one's own nose—whatever shape or color it may be.

"That is not to say there is no friction here, for one sees bitterness and unrest just as elsewhere. How can you have change without such things? But I think Hawaiians more than most were born and brought up as companions of change, not so much in themselves as in the people and life around them. Perhaps now change does not come so hard to them."

Talk turned to the East-West Center itself and its effectiveness as a cultural bridge across the Pacific.

"Academically, we are part of the university," explained Masao Takahashi, a young language scholar from Japan. "To be truthful, my country has universities that are better, but they have something else, too—students who are strictly Japanese. The real value here is outside the classroom." He gestured politely around the table. "My friends come from countries that Japan cannot live without, although in the past we have not known each other well enough. It seems curious, but I have come all the way to Hawaii to meet my own neighbors."

For Mohammed Yusuf Salehi, 21, a political-science major from Afghanistan, the center's value is largely a matter of perspective.

"I think sometimes I have learned more here about my own country," he said, "than about anyone else's. If there is a student riot in my city of Kabul, Felix or Masao naturally asks me, 'What's that all about?' Well, I have been in these riots and so I tell my view —we young Afghans want our government to provide a decent education and job opportunities for our people. The government listens to our suggestions, but it does not always act. So the students can only retaliate by demonstrating, sometimes causing the university to close its doors.

"But while I am explaining," Yusuf continued, "Felix looks puzzled and finally he asks, 'You mean you would rather have *no* education than part of one?' So I think to myself, these Samoans, they are nice people but they sometimes miss the point. Then later I wonder just who has missed the point. And finally I realize that it is difficult to have perspective close to home, even when you feel certain you are in the right. And perhaps Felix has taught me something about my own Afghanistan."

Parade rest: At Aloha Week's festivities in October a small watcher hangs on to his balloon as the bands march by.

The same concern for other people's problems now and then occupies Henry and Lillian Risk. Henry and Lillian, however, don't tackle just any problem. They are specialists in recovering lost or buried treasure.

I met them one evening during a walk along the water's edge at Waikiki, when the crowds and the activity had subsided for the day and the beach had regained a faint touch of that haunting quality once described by a young Britisher, Rupert Brooke, in his poem, "Waikiki":

> *And new stars burn into the ancient skies,*
> *Over the murmurous soft Hawaiian sea.*

Admittedly there is little left to call haunting about Waikiki today, and more often than not Brooke's murmurous soft Hawaiian sea is lost in the sound of murmurous soft Hawaiian music—played at ear-splitting level by hotel and nightclub bands. And yet there is something irresistible about the beach itself, with its pale crescent of well-manicured sand, its hotel terraces opening on the water, and its distant line of surfers and outriggers darting like shuttles across the green loom of the sea.

For a time I walked alone just back of the water, past quiet groups of young people in the deliberately ragged dress that marks them collectively, and usually unfairly, as hippies. It was here among the half shadows that I found Henry and Lillian, though for a moment I had the impression of a World War II demolition team clearing a mine field.

They were stationed a dozen yards apart and moving slowly across the sand, each holding what looked like a mop handle with a giant dinner plate attached at an angle to its lower end. As they walked they swung the plates back and forth in narrow arcs before them, half an inch or so above the sand.

As I drew nearer, I noticed that both wore earphones and that they seemed oblivious to everything around them, including occasional passersby who attempted conversation. I recognized the mop-handle-dinner-plate affairs as metal detectors, instruments used increasingly by souvenir hunters for such items as buried shell fragments and bullets on Civil War battlefields.

Rather than disturb what was plainly another kind of hunt, I waited until Henry and Lillian decided to take a break and then introduced myself. We shook hands, and they told me what they were after.

"Anything people drop that gets buried in the sand," explained Lillian, a lively and charming woman in her early 40's. "Of course it has to be metal—the detectors don't register wood or plastic—but that means everything from pennies and the little tabs off pop-top soda cans to diamond rings and parts of automobile engines. You'd be surprised what people bring to the beach."

Bozo the Clown shakes hands with young admirers. Aloha Week, begun in 1947, combines street carnival, the pageantry of old Hawaii, flowers, music, and bursts of color.

In fact there are a number of surprises to Henry's and Lillian's hobby, such as the revelation that for hard cash, meaning coins, the sands in front of luxury hotels are a poor prospect.

"They're more for the occasional wristwatch or fancy compact," Henry said. "As a rule, wealthy tourists don't bother with cash; they simply charge beach expenses to their hotel bills. For coins the best bet is the public area, where the drink stands and the rented surfboards are."

I asked what an average night's harvest there came to, and Lillian answered, "It all depends on the phase of the moon." Then she caught my guarded look and burst out laughing.

"No, we're not cranks or mystics," she said. "It's just that beach sand follows the wash of the tide, and anything underneath moves with it. The heavier tides seem to scour the bottom offshore and bring up the most items along with the sand. Which means a full moon is the best time for

Aboard a float wreathed in blooms, a warrior dressed in ancient style presides over hula dancers and musicians. The theme of 1969's Aloha Week centered on music. Honolulu resounded with guitars, bands, singing, and everywhere the strains of the song "Aloha Oe," composed by Queen Liliuokalani. The royal couple chosen for the event, King Kamalulani and beplumed Queen Leilani (right), raise their glasses for a toast at the banquet; in the Royal Hawaiian Hotel a young man in formal island dress leads his partner at the ball.

electronic beachcombing. But to answer your question, I'd say we average two dollars in change on the nights we go out. It's not what you'd call a profit-making venture, we just enjoy it."

I asked what they collected besides coins, and Lillian threw up her hands. "Come and look through our storage boxes! Costume jewelry, manicure scissors, cigarette lighters, campaign buttons—you name it, and Henry probably has it tucked away somewhere."

With truly valuable items, I learned, Henry and Lillian generally manage to locate the owners—most often through hotels nearest to the area of the find. "Sometimes when a guest loses something valuable," Henry said, "his hotel will give us a call. I work for a construction company during the day, but if either one of us is available, we're glad to help. I don't know how many room keys we've found in a year's time and turned in to front desks."

Most finds aren't worth the considerable trouble of trying to return them, and more than one Risk family friend has an attractive cigarette lighter or compact as an unwitting gift from Waikiki. Henry and Lillian have kept only two valuable items themselves after failing to find the owners. One is a Spanish silver coin dated 1796, and the other a man's gold watch worth about $260.

After a while Henry donned his earphones again and set off on a new search. "You can use the detectors with or without the phones," Lillian said, "but we usually wear them to discourage interruptions—you can sort of ignore people that way without being rude. During breaks, however, we're only too happy to answer questions. Here, try these on."

She adjusted the phones over my ears and made a series of sweeps around us with the detector plate. At first I heard only a low steady hum, but presently it jumped an octave or two and began wavering. I turned the phones over to Lillian and before long she had the target pinpointed. Unhooking a small wire mesh basket from her belt, she scooped and sifted the sand several times and came up with a 1963 penny.

"Risk Family Rule Number One," she said, passing it to me with a curtsy. Then she reached down and picked up a battered paper cup, dropping it in the nearest trash bin. "Rule Number Two, or something—it's everybody's beach to enjoy, and look after."

On the next break I said goodbye to Henry and Lillian and asked when I might find them out on the beach again.

"Next week we've got two teen-age sons home on vacation," Lillian said, "and I imagine we won't see the detectors for a while. The boys like to take them out at all hours, even though they lose money at it."

That seemed impossible, and Lillian smiled.

"They don't waste their time looking for *things*," she said. "They're hunting for *dates*. There's hardly a cute young number alive who can watch a boy go by with one of these things and not ask what it's all about. To younger members of the Risk family these aren't metal detectors, they're 'icebreakers.' And they cost a pretty penny in movies and sundaes." She held out her hand.

"Maybe Henry and I could meet you for a dip one day soon. I'm told the water's lovely."

Aglow in the evening, the new State Capitol combines a look of balance with airiness. The fluted crown, rising above an open court, suggests the islands' volcanic origin. Once the focus of a sleepy town dotted with taro patches, this area now throbs with city life. But plans for a park here from sea to mountains will preserve for all the sweeping beauty of Kamehameha's land.

Kaneohe Bay

Koolau Range

Waianae Range

Honolulu

Diamond Head

OAHU

Pearl Harbor, Polynesian villages, cannonading surf

O'AHU MAKA 'EWA 'EWA, runs an old Hawaiian adage — "Unfriendly are the eyes of the people of Oahu."

The saying originated with a disgruntled goddess who visited Oahu, but mortals are always welcome. Today the number runs to well over a million outsiders a year, or 85 percent of those who visit the 50th State. The wonder is that with only 607.7 square miles to do it in, Oahu still preserves a touch of paradise.

Those who complain that Oahu's paradise wears a dollar sign generally have seen little more of the island than its commercial heart — central Honolulu and Waikiki. Here, indeed, the crush of tourists is so massive that it overwhelms even the local businessmen. "If everybody decided to come to the beach for dinner on a particular night," says a Waikiki hotel manager wryly, "the island would capsize."

Certainly Oahu has a lopsided look in terms of population. The great urban galaxy of Honolulu on the southeastern coast accounts for 371,000 Oahuans, more than half of the island's permanent residents and nearly one out of every two Hawaiians. Yet elsewhere much of Oahu is as

Exploding from the surface at her trainer's hand signal, a false killer whale hurtles 24 feet to snatch fish at Oahu's Sea Life Park. The 20-acre preserve exhibits new ways of tapping the resources of Hawaii's playground — the sea.

sparsely settled as matching areas of the so-called Neighbor Islands.

To the despair of publicity men Oahu resists nicknames, including such suggestions as the "Aloha Island"—few but the travel guides use it. Other sources insist on translating Oahu's Polynesian name as "the gathering place," although, as in the case of Hawaii itself, no one really knows the original meaning of the word.

One of the older links in the Hawaiian chain, having thrust above the sea some 3.4 million years ago, Oahu at one stage was two separate volcanic islands that eventually fused during the course of millenniums into a single mass. Even today the island bears witness to its dual origin, lifting two parallel mountain ranges—Koolau on the east and Waianae in the west—like a pair of immense windbreaks against the trades.

Not all of Oahu took eons to materialize. Volcanologists estimate that the island's most famous feature, the giant crater known to early Polynesians as *Leahi* ("place of fire") and to later generations as Diamond Head, may have been forged by volcanic action within a matter of weeks, possibly even days. Erosion then set to work, filing great notches in the crater rim and etching away the smooth slopes with narrow ravines until the headland today suggests the shattered remnant of some enormous seashell cast up and abandoned by the tide.

Less famous yet infinitely more spectacular is Oahu's Nuuanu Pali—literally, "cool-height cliff"—a dizzying escarpment of the Koolau Range that soars as high as 3,150 feet at one point on the east coast, stripping the incoming winds of moisture and turning leeward Waikiki and surrounding areas into a sunbather's sheltered paradise.

Contestants hear instructions during the 1969 Duke Kahanamoku Hawaiian Surfing Classic. Named for the Olympic swimming champion of 1912 and 1920 whose world tours helped popularize surfing, the annual meet takes place wherever the greatest waves thunder onto Oahu.

Oahu, however, is much more than mere scenery; for one thing it is people like Casey Coryell. Casey is 17, very pretty, and her real name is Katherine; the nickname results from her initials, K. C.

I met Casey through her parents, Roger and Ernestine Coryell, at a party in their home in Hawaii Kai, a new community east of Diamond Head. Casey and I fell to discussing traditional Hawaiian sports, such as surfing and ti-leaf sliding. The latter is a technique of careering down a muddy slope with a cluster of giant leaves from the ti plant as the toboggan. I asked Casey if young Hawaiians still practiced the sport.

"Yes," she answered, "but you can only do it during fall and winter rains, when the hills are good and slick. Fluming's much better, because you can do that all year round."

Fluming? Casey smiled. "That's what we call it in the islands. Flumes are the big irrigation ditches that carry water down out of the mountains to the lowland cane and pineapple fields. To flume, all you do is hop in the ditch, float on your back, and catch a free ride partway down with the water. In some places you can even float through tunnels in the mountains and ride aqueducts over the valleys. It's a great sport."

And where, I asked, would one find a likely ditch, or rather flume? "Up in the Koolau Range," Casey explained. "Most of the valleys there have flumes in them, but you have to know the way because some are fenced off and others. . . . What are you doing next Saturday?"

And so on a memorable Saturday I went fluming with Casey, her father and mother, a smaller sister Carol, and two young men from the neighborhood. Driving north along the windward coast in two cars, we followed the lush corridor of cane fields and pastures running between the sea and the great upturned saw blade of the Koolau Range.

Like many another breathtaking spot in Hawaii, the Koolau memorializes a grim chapter of island history. In a deep notch of the Nuuanu Pali escarpment in 1795, with an invading army from the Island of Hawaii, the great warrior chieftain Kamehameha I met and defeated the forces of Oahu under their king, Kalanikupule. According to legend, several hundred of the surviving Oahuans leaped or were driven over the sheer face of Nuuanu Pali to their death more than 200 feet below.

Some accounts say the victorious Kamehameha treated his conquered rival with typical Polynesian chivalry by having his brains clubbed out as a gesture to the gods—a practice that helps explain the high incidence of suicide among defeated Hawaiian warriors.

The battle at Nuuanu Pali had at least one beneficial result. It solidified Kamehameha's grip over most of the islands and gave Hawaii its first unified rule in more than a thousand years of history.

Beyond the small coastal town of Kaaawa we turned inland through a valley richly carpeted to a thickness of 10 or 12 feet by sugarcane. The irrigation flumes plainly were at peak operation, for within a mile the dirt road became a quagmire. We parked the cars on a raised embankment and slogged westward through mud toward the Koolau.

Once on higher ground we entered the luxuriant forest typical of the windward slopes of Hawaii's mountains. Though the morning was cloudless, the trail lay deep in shadow beneath a canopy of wild banana, eucalyptus, ironwood, guava, and hibiscus shrubs as tall as giant boxwoods.

Along the way Roger Coryell pointed out trees as unfamiliar to me as they were vital to the early Hawaiians—*koa,* from which the hulls of the great ocean-going canoes were fashioned; *hau,* the traditional wood used for the outriggers; and *'ulu,* or breadfruit, whose sap served as a binder with coconut fiber for the final caulking.

"Once they had the hull as tight as they could make it," Roger said, "they launched it and held a ceremony called 'drinking the sea.' A group of people got on each side of the canoe and rocked it back and forth until the caulking and the fiber lashings were drenched and started to swell, making everything snug and watertight."

Equally important to life ashore was the *kukui,* or candlenut tree, which we encountered in scattered stands along the trail. As the name suggests, early Hawaiians used the oily nuts as miniature torches after first drying

Portrait of "the Duke," displayed at Duke Kahanamoku's, a Waikiki Beach nightclub, gazes past the perpetual trophy of the surfing contest bearing his name.

them in the sun. The oil also served as a remedy for stomach ailments. So important were candlenuts as a source of illumination that the Hawaiian word for light itself is *kukui.*

"Even today," Roger said, "many older Hawaiians call the ordinary household lamp *kukui uila* — 'electric candlenut.'"

As the trail steepened, Casey and Ernestine gradually dropped behind with young Carol, and I began to suspect that the hike was too much for a girl of eight. But I hadn't reckoned on Hawaiian custom. After a while Roger and I paused beside the path with Casey's two friends, Paul and John. Presently Ernestine, Casey, and Carol caught up, each carrying an assortment of leis and small wreaths made of vines interwoven with wild flowers, mainly ginger. After the proper ceremony of decorating the menfolk we all turned once more up the trail.

The flume was everything Casey had promised, in addition to being a work of art. Three miles up the mountain we rounded a bend in the path and came on a great groove carved in the slope, beautifully squared and lined with expertly masoned stone. The inner width of the flume was roughly four feet and the depth two and a half, with the lining so smooth that an immense volume of water slipped along it almost unbroken by ripples.

Some 40 yards upcurrent the flume issued from a gaping tunnel in a shoulder of the mountain, and at an equal distance downstream it took off across a deep gorge on an aqueduct supported by a trestle.

For the day Casey had recommended hiking clothes over the oldest available bathing suit. "The flumes look smooth," she had warned, "but where you bump the bottom, you may find a few surprises in the cement work."

There was no stopping point between the mouth of the tunnel and a spot well out on the aqueduct, where heavy beams had been bolted at intervals across the top of the flume for support. John noted that the water level was unusually high, leaving mere inches of clearance under the beams.

"Keep flat, with your head back when you reach them," he recommended, "then pick the beam you want beforehand. As soon as you grab it get your shoulders above the surface to reduce the drag; otherwise, you'll create a dam and the water will back up on you and push harder."

We started our first run just below the mouth of the tunnel, with John leading off and the rest of the flumers following a few yards apart — myself, then Paul, and finally Casey. While awaiting my turn I discovered it was possible to stand upright in the flume with water churning above knee level. But once a flumer sits down, he is launched and committed.

Scuba diver jumps into Waimanalo Bay (right) to guide the underwater habitat Aegir *into position on the seabed. Developed at the Makapuu Oceanic Center, the craft can house six explorers at depths to 580 feet for as long as 20 days. Above, a diver glides near the* Aegir *during tests 70 feet underwater.*

John took off with a splash and went sailing downstream at a good clip feet first, with only his blond head showing. Then I was in the stinging cold of the water and bobbing along behind, waving cheerfully to Carol, who stayed behind with her parents. For a time I enjoyed the dappled effect of branches sweeping by overhead and then I was out in bright sunlight high over the gorge. The sensation was pleasant and I idly surveyed my toes, showing just above water ahead of me like a disembodied cow-catcher. Something beyond them caught my attention, and I was suddenly faced with a wooden beam rushing toward me at eye level.

My first thought was that the water in the flume must have risen, for there seemed no clearance at all under the beam. I drew a quick breath and prepared to submerge, wondering just how many beams I could avoid before I had to surface — and catch the next beam like a Hawaiian war club in the head. Just then I got a glimpse of blond hair some yards downstream and realized that John had slipped safely under the barrier. Reassured, I tilted my head back and watched half a dozen beams flash past uncomfortably close to my nose. Then I put up both hands, caught hold of the seventh beam, and lifted my shoulders free of the surface. The movement broke the water's grip and I was soon on top of the beam, ready to walk back along the aqueduct for another run.

We made more than a dozen of them, pushing our starting point as far as we dared into the pitch black and rush of water in the tunnel. As Casey had prophesied, I found the bottom of the flume studded with tiny pinpoints of concrete, and before long I had shredded the seat of my swimming trunks. The truth is I shredded a bit more than that, but in Hawaii we never discuss fluming scars.

Finally the chill of the water drove us out and we hiked down the mountain, gathering armloads of wild ginger for friends of the Coryells. On the return drive we stopped at a grove of trees beside a beach, and Ernestine spread a banquet of chicken, fresh pineapple, and wine. Afterward we spent an hour on the sand, letting the sun bake away the lingering effects of icy mountain water, and reached home in the late afternoon.

It had been a day far removed from the usual run of sightseeing excursions, and one that still makes me think of Oahu as Casey's island.

Jagen Lal, for one, would dispute the claim, even though he's a relative newcomer to Oahu. I met Jagen one evening near the village of Laie on the island's north coast, where he was preparing to go to war with the enemies of Fiji. The preparations were impressive and I'm sure the Fijians would have won, but then they had to turn the stage over to a group of Tahitian women dancers.

Jagen and his fellow warriors are part of the cast of the Polynesian Cultural Center, a major attraction on Oahu inspired and directed by members of the Church of Jesus Christ of Latter-day Saints. The center is an offshoot of the Mormon missionary college at Laie and it serves a dual purpose: It offers a living museum for half a dozen ancient Pacific cultures, and it provides income for tuition and expenses to students at the college, many of whom come from distant islands of the South Pacific.

I met Jagen backstage after the spectacular nightly performance of dances based on the traditions of Hawaii, Fiji, Samoa, Tonga, Tahiti, and

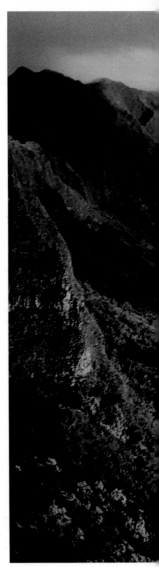

Flutings eroded by rain-fed waterfalls ripple the face of the Pali, the great cliff that stretches 22 miles along windward Oahu. Pounding waves carved the nearly vertical rampart as the sea level rose eons ago. When the sea receded, volcanic rock on the valley floor began weathering into soil. "The ... quiet valley spread out like a map beneath our feet," wrote missionary Hiram Bingham, "its vast amphitheatre of mountains, and beyond it, the heaving, white fringed ocean, rising in the distance ... make a powerful impression on the senses."

Maori New Zealand. Earlier I had visited the adjoining collection of villages representing the same cultures, where other students demonstrate the distinctive but related customs of all six peoples.

To me, Jagen and his fellow students seemed something of a contradiction. On the one hand they were attempting to preserve the colorful but fading customs of early Polynesia. On the other they were studying the Western culture and technology that threaten to extinguish those customs altogether, as has happened to a large degree in Hawaii. I asked Jagen if he didn't feel a sense of conflict.

"Yes," he answered, "but not in the way you imagine. For me it is more a matter of competition." He waved toward the darkened stage and the villages beyond it. "Every afternoon and evening I am surrounded by the culture not only of Fiji but also of others related to us. I am not so foolish as to admire everything I see, but what is good I accept, and I remember. In the mornings I do the same with what your people have to offer, and if I have some wisdom I choose well from both.

"That was not always the way with us," he continued. "In the past there was such a gulf between Fijians and the outside world that we tended to accept everything from it, or nothing. Either way we failed. Here at Laie, as Western students but still as Fijians, we can learn what you have in the West that truly suits us, what may change but not destroy us as a people. And that is what we will take home.

"Meanwhile," he added, smiling, "if you enjoyed the performance then we have taught you something, too—that a world without Fijians would be a little poorer."

At least one aspect of Polynesian culture has flourished in contact with the West. Throughout half the world today, wherever there are beaches and ocean swells, somebody is probably practicing the traditional Hawaiian art of *he'e nalu*—"wave-sliding" —better known as surfing. Hawaiians boast the finest consistently ridable surf in the world, a claim readily acknowledged by everyone except Californians, Australians, South Africans, Malaysians, and perhaps a few others. Yet the fact remains that the most famous surfing competitions take place on Oahu's northern and western coasts, at such renowned beaches as Makaha and Sunset.

ROGER H. CORYELL

Ducking under the beams of an aqueduct, Casey Coryell introduces the author to the sport of fluming— hitching a ride down a flume, or irrigation canal, that carries water from the mountains to lowland fields.

Oahuans have other surfing beaches with such grizzly names as Suicides, Point Panic, Banzai Pipeline, and Pounders; but Makaha and Sunset are the ones usually chosen for the great international meets.

The average visitor to Hawaii thinks of surfing strictly in terms of Waikiki, and in fact it is an ideal beach for learning the sport. During my stay in Honolulu, I took a memorable hour's lesson with a part-Hawaiian named Jesse Crawford, an excellent instructor and the beach captain for one of Waikiki's finest hotels, appropriately called the Surfrider.

Jesse showed the same skill with me that has transformed such novices as television actress Lucille Ball and her children into creditable surfers —after somewhat more than an hour's instruction. By the end of the lesson he had me standing more or less upright on the board and riding small waves for triumphant stretches of a hundred yards.

"You're doing fine, just fine," Jesse said generously as we paddled back to shore, "though you're not quite ready for Makaha."

The truth is I never will be except in summer, when Makaha is practically a millpond. From May through October whatever real surf Oahu has comes from the south as a result of Antarctica's winter storms, and the famous beaches on the island's north side are barren of surfers. Beginning in late November, however, it is the Arctic's turn. Storms bred in the Aleutians lash the northern Pacific into a winter fury, sending monstrous swells driving southward on a collision course with Hawaii. Then there is thunder all along Oahu's northern coast and only the very skillful, or the very foolish, put out from shore.

One of the former is 39-year-old George Downing, three times winner of the International Surfing Championships (Makaha), a yearly classic that draws the world's finest surfers to Hawaii. I spent an evening discussing surfing with George at Waikiki's venerable Outrigger Canoe Club, famous since its founding in 1908 for champion surfers and outrigger canoe teams. I learned that to Hawaiians "ridable surf" may mean waves up to 35 feet in height, but that size is only one factor.

"It depends on how the wave breaks, or 'cracks,' as surfers put it," George began. "Many beaches in the world have 35-foot waves. But what gives Hawaii's surf that special quality is the underwater barricade of coral reefs that breaks the swells up as they come in, so that a wave doesn't crack all at once but 'peels' across its face in a continuing motion—like a row of dominoes when you push it over. That moving edge just in front of the white water is called the 'shoulder,' and that's where you get the speed, as well as the long ride."

Speed, it developed, can mean as much as 40 miles an hour, an impressive thought to the layman. "It's no problem as long as you're up," George assured me, "but when you have a spill, or a 'wipe-out,' you have to dig in fast." I asked him to explain.

"You have to dig into the wave itself," George said. "With a 30-footer, you can't afford to let it crack right on you; it would be like standing inside a three-story house when it collapses. In a wipe-out at 40 miles an hour you tend to skid down the slope of the wave, and if you keep on skidding you'll be right underneath when that part of it cracks. So the minute you hit the water you reach back with one arm and literally claw your way into the wave to slow down. Then you burrow in fast and try to get to the other side."

Another, though actually very minor, problem to surfing in Hawaii's waters is the presence now and then of sharks. The dangers are more psychological than real, for in the last decade only one fatality due to sharks has been reported among surfers.

George told me he had encountered sharks a number of times in his career. "But as a rule," he said, "they clear out when they see you. If they

Torches blaze fiery arcs about a dancer performing the nifo oti, *a Samoan feat of skill, at the Polynesian Cultural Center in the village of Laie. Established by the Mormon Church to perpetuate Pacific cultures, the center displays handicrafts and music in six villages: Hawaiian, Tongan, Samoan, Maori, Fijian, and Tahitian. At left, an outrigger carries Maori dancers on the center's lagoon in the Pageant of the Long Canoes. At the Hawaiian village Emma Kahawaii demonstrates her quilting skill; missionaries introduced the craft.*

don't, it's well to look for another beach. Once or twice I've surfed into a school of them by accident." Horrified, I asked what he had done.

"Just said, 'Excuse me,' and surfed right on through," he answered grinning. "But I'll say this: It was no time for a wipe-out."

Not long afterward I thought enviously of George and his quick departure from *manō,* as Hawaiians call the shark. Not that I was in any real danger, according to Ken Taylor, and Ken has been dealing with manō for years. He had invited me to go scuba diving off Makaha in early autumn before the surf had begun to build. Ken's 17-year-old daughter Theresa, his frequent partner, decided to accompany us.

In addition to being an expert commercial diver, Ken runs a thriving business in Honolulu called Coral Fish Hawaii, which supplies exotic reef specimens by air to mainland collectors. Ken had a number of orders to fill, and we set off one early morning in an outboard from the town of Waianae on Oahu's west side, turning north along the coast toward Kaena Point. Once again I was impressed by the clarity of Hawaii's coastal waters; occasionally Ken stopped to survey the bottom, and I found I could make out the shapes of coral reefs and even some of the brighter colors of marine life 40 feet below us. Finally Ken anchored in 30 feet of water above a reef half a mile off Makaha, and he and Theresa and I went over the side with scuba gear and the collecting equipment.

Ken's method of trapping specimens was simple but highly effective. At the base of the reef he uncoiled a net woven of transparent nylon filament, 60 feet long and 10 feet wide. One long edge of the net was weighted down by lead sinkers, and the opposite edge was buoyed with small plastic floats. When stretched out, the entire affair formed an almost invisible fence across the ocean floor.

Ken arranged the net at a right angle against the reef and signaled Theresa and me to follow him along the massive hedgerow of coral, its somber limbs festooned with bright garlands of browsing fish that drifted slowly back and forth with the metronome surge of the sea.

Some 30 yards from the net Ken divided up the rest of the gear: a pair of small hand nets each for himself and Theresa, a plastic collecting box with a spring-secured lid for me. And then the drive began.

Swimming a yard or two apart and hugging the wall of the reef, we slowly herded clusters of glittering fish before us, as though sweeping a jumble of stained-glass fragments across the sea floor. In the swirling mass ahead I picked out dazzling combinations—magenta with gold, turquoise mixed with silver, indigo and orange, black and scarlet.

As we approached the net, Ken motioned me to swing wide toward the outer edge, while he and Theresa coaxed the main body of fish head-on into the webbing. Silent pandemonium followed as the cornered fish lunged frantically and repeatedly against the barrier. Ken and Theresa selected the valuable ones, gently scooping them up with the hand nets and expertly transferring them to my collecting box. We carefully freed other fish still caught in the net, then headed back for another drive.

Three passes netted some two dozen specimens of the types Ken was after; we coiled up the net and made for the surface. Back aboard the boat Ken transferred the catch to a 25-gallon drum at the stern and

Packing colorful reef fish to ship to the mainland, Ken Taylor slips them into plastic bags of sea water for his shop, Coral Fish Hawaii.

identified a few varieties for me by their popular names—yellow tangs, spotted puffers, Moorish idols, damsels, and longnose butterflyfish.

"These are good reefs," Ken said after we had weighed anchor and headed southwestward toward another likely spot. "They'll stay that way, too, as long as we don't overfish them and nobody gives them a shot of bleach." I didn't follow him and Ken explained an illegal method of fishing that amounts to wholesale slaughter.

"It's a technique used for food fish," Ken said, "and it has the advantage of being dirt cheap. All it takes is a 60-cent plastic bottle of bleach, and no regard for life. You simply dive with the bottle on a reef where fish are concentrated and swim along, squeezing the bottle as you go. Within 20 minutes or so every living thing in the area is paralyzed and dying. So you pick what you want and leave the other 99 percent behind—starfish, sea snails, shrimp, the colorful little fish nobody eats, even the reef itself, which will probably die, too, or be a wasteland for a long time.

"The food fish don't seem to be spoiled for human consumption," he added. "They're just as tasty as if they were caught with a net or a hook and line. But everything else dies along with them."

"Don't misunderstand," Theresa added quietly. "Ninety-nine out of a hundred fishermen in our islands are decent people, and they know that without the reef they're minus a job—just as collectors and surfers are hurt when coral's wiped out. The problem is to educate that one man in a hundred. Or if you can't educate him, to keep him ashore."

For the next dive Ken chose a reef 50 feet down and a mile off the southern end of Makaha. We set the net as before and made the first run, catching a few worthwhile specimens plus a number of curious small fish that made a clearly audible "beep-beep" sound when they became tangled in the webbing. Automatically I began to free them, and Theresa's hand suddenly was on mine.

Banded Moorish idols, yellow tangs, and a longnose butterflyfish flit amid neighbors in a Ken Taylor aquarium.

At first I thought the strange fish must be valuable and that I was meant to collect them, but Theresa gave no sign and only stared evenly at me through her face plate. I turned to look for Ken and then realized why she had caught my hand: With his only weapons, the hand nets, Ken was driving at an eight-foot shark less than 20 feet away. For a long second the shark stood its ground, then swung away into the lengthening shadows of the open sea. Only then did Theresa release my hand and motion upward with her thumb, the signal to surface. Ken swept up the net and followed us to the boat.

I learned then what had happened. The curious small fish entangled in the net were *weke,* or goatfish, whose distress calls carry a great distance underwater. Alerted to a possible meal, the shark had homed on the sound, gliding in from the sea like a gray wraith toward our net. For nearly a minute he had coasted along within 10 feet of me, awaiting a chance at the helpless fish. And, novice that I was, I hadn't noticed him.

Presently Ken and Theresa had seen the danger. Unsure of how I might react when I saw it, too, Theresa had seized my hand while Ken went for the shark.

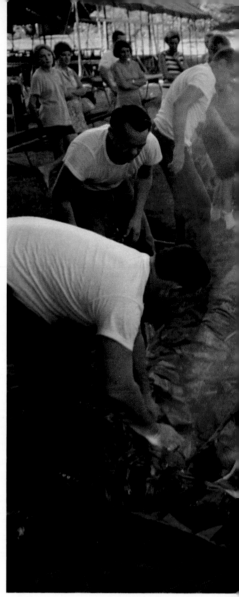

Feasts fit for ancient Hawaiian kings, luaus today often combine fund-raising with fun and food. In preparation for a community-center benefit, volunteers (left) lift heated rocks from an imu, or pit oven, then stuff them into the carcasses of pigs. Wire baskets of sweet potatoes cook in the pit overnight with the pigs, sealed under layers of wet ti and banana leaves, burlap, canvas, and earth (above). Next morning children savor the mouth-watering aroma (right).

"Probably he was more curious than hungry," Ken said in a matter-of-fact way, "but you can never be 100 percent sure. And we didn't know how you'd take to your first shark at close range."

My guess is, roughly the same way I would take to my second one. But I'm in no great hurry to find out.

Driving back toward Honolulu, we passed a gigantic notch in the Waianae Range known as Kolekole Pass. Here, according to Hawaiian legend, a goddess stands guard against intruders. Most Oahuans agree that she must have been asleep in the early hours of December 7, 1941. For it was through Kolekole Pass that the main assault wave of Japanese carrier planes swept in a surprise attack on the U. S. naval base at Pearl Harbor, touching off a war that was to last four terrible years and span the world's largest ocean as though in mockery of its name—Pacific.

Nearly three decades after the Japanese attack, Pearl Harbor still ranks second only to Waikiki Beach as Oahu's top tourist attraction. What the visitor sees today is a vast base no longer on the outer rim of American defenses in the Pacific but nonetheless a vital link with them all.

"Without Hawaii we'd be crippled throughout Asia," Admiral John S. McCain, Jr., U. S. Commander in Chief Pacific, told me one day in his office overlooking Pearl Harbor. "Some people insist that nuclear missiles and long-range submarines have made forward bases like Hawaii obsolete—until they start remembering names like Korea and Viet Nam, where the man with the rifle still decides the final outcome."

He waved through the window at the crowded docks and repair yards of Pearl Harbor and beyond, to the equally busy flight lines of Hickam Air Force Base.

"These islands are more than a threshold on the Pacific; they're the gate, the lock, the key, all in one."

Certainly the Japanese took the same view on that long-ago Sunday morning in December of 1941, for they set out to smash the gate beyond repair. In the space of two hours they all but destroyed it, launching carrier-based strikes not only against Pearl Harbor, but also against Hickam Air Force Base (then known as Hickam Field), the Army's Schofield Barracks, Wheeler Field, the U. S. Marine Corps' air station at Kaneohe Bay (then a naval air station), and the smaller fields at Ewa and Bellows.

In the end the gate held, but at fearful cost to the United States: eight battleships damaged or destroyed, with the loss of 10 other combat and support vessels; 2,403 American lives extinguished; 188 aircraft in ruins; and American power in the Pacific crippled, if not shattered, for months to come. Only the Navy's submarine fleet and three aircraft carriers, the

Plant breeder checks sugarcane at the Kailua Experiment Station of the Hawaiian Sugar Planters' Association. Above, the sun warms methyl alcohol in the black bulb of a "wig-wag"; expanding gas forces the liquid through the arm, making a bulb at the other end heavier. The arm pivots, moving a lever to record the intensity and duration of sunlight—more sun means more sugar.

Tugs escort the aircraft carrier Ranger, *her deck bristling with planes, out of Pearl Harbor as she departs for*

December 7, 1941: "A date which will live in infamy," said President Franklin D. Roosevelt after the Japanese surprise attack on Pearl Harbor; 2,403 Americans died, more than 1,100 of them aboard the Arizona. *Smoke and flames billow from the* West Virginia *(foreground) and the* Tennessee *as a Navy rescue boat cruises the waters near "Battleship Row."*

Southeast Asia. The gleaming memorial to the battleship Arizona *(upper right) lies off the tip of Ford Island.*

NATIONAL GEOGRAPHIC PHOTOGRAPHERS JAMES L. AMOS (ABOVE) AND BATES LITTLEHALES

Navy officer conducts a memorial service at the simple concrete-and-marble shrine above the Arizona. The battered hulk of the battleship still rests where she blew up about 8:00 that Sunday morning and sank at her berth. In permanent tribute to the crewmen who remain entombed aboard, an honor guard raises and lowers a flag over her, morning and evening.

Air Force pararescue men search for a mock-up of an Apollo spacecraft as their plane turns out to sea over Oahu during a recovery exercise. Their objective sighted, the men float down (right). Trained medics as well as parachutists and divers, the men also jump to the aid of vessels with sick or injured crewmen, and search for survivors of ship-wrecks and downed aircraft.

latter then at sea on maneuvers, escaped to strike a later counterblow.

The cruelest loss of all lies unrecovered on the floor of Pearl Harbor. A graceful marble memorial crowns the sunken superstructure of the battleship U.S.S. *Arizona,* demolished by a chain of explosions that reached her magazines. In a unique gesture the Navy decided to leave the bodies of more than 1,100 of her crew entombed forever where they had died gallantly, and almost instantly, with their ship.

Amid overwhelming tragedy there were moments of redeeming humor. One Navy survivor of the attack, James J. Downs, today is an automobile salesman in Honolulu. In 1941 "J.J.," as friends call him, was a 19-year-old seaman aboard the destroyer U.S.S. *Blue,* one of the few ships out of 96 in Pearl Harbor that managed to get under way and into action during the raid. With less than a third of her normal 146-man crew aboard, the *Blue* shot down five attacking planes and probably sank a Japanese midget submarine, one of five launched by mother subs off the coast of Oahu. The *Blue's* exploits earned her a unit citation, one of the earliest awarded in World War II.

For J.J. Downs the Japanese attack had unique personal significance, a significance he explained to me one day at the Navy Chief Petty Officers' Club in Pearl Harbor.

"The night before the attack," J.J. said, "that is, Saturday, December 6, I had a date with a Japanese girl in Honolulu. But that afternoon ashore I met a dazzling Hawaiian-Dutch girl, and the hours just seemed to slip by.

"Well, I'll be honest with you," he said, "I did a terrible thing. I stood the Japanese girl up and took the Hawaiian-Dutch girl out instead. Then the very next morning there I am, back aboard the *Blue,* and here comes half the Imperial Japanese Navy Air Force, fighting mad. And I said to myself, 'J.J., let this be a lesson to you.'"

In another way it was also a lesson to the attackers. At the moment of victory the leader of the Japanese air armada, Comdr. Mitsuo Fuchida, made a disturbing observation: Despite the completeness of the surprise, American gun crews on the warships in Pearl Harbor recovered from the shock with astonishing speed and got their antiaircraft batteries into swift and deadly operation. The American reaction would become a familiar one to the Japanese before war's end.

To the great satisfaction of Hawaiians the only midget submarines that patrol their waters today are devoted to advancing man's peaceful knowledge of the deep. One such craft, a bubble-like research submarine capable of carrying two men down to 300 feet, operates out of Oahu's internationally known Makapuu Oceanic Center, just east of Diamond Head.

The center is a pioneer force in Hawaii's growing specialty, oceanography and related marine sciences. Much of what it learns, as well as captures, from the deep benefits Oahuans and tourists alike at the center's oceanarium, Sea Life Park. Among the center's other attractions are a revolutionary underwater habitat called *Aegir* (after a Scandinavian sea god), a rapidly developing deep-sea test and research range, and an extremely likable genius by the name of Dr. Kenneth Norris.

Ken Norris is director of the center's research organization, known as the Oceanic Institute, and an authority on the sperm whale. Friends had told me of his plan to capture a young whale alive, and I called at the institute to learn more about the project. Ken sat me down in an empty classroom in front of a blackboard and proceeded to describe some of the wonders of what clearly is his passion in life.

"Here," he began, sketching the rough outline of a sperm whale on the board, "is a beast designed from the keel up by a committee. Not just an ordinary committee, mind you, but an *interdepartmental* committee. You wouldn't believe the complicated plumbing in it."

I might believe it if I could really understand it, but that's not important; what matters are the results of the plumbing. I learned, for example, that sperm whales have been recorded at depths as great as 3,600 feet, where pressure is more than 100 times that at sea level.

"Yet the sperm whale goes merrily along," Ken said, "sounding and surfacing, often at considerable speed, in a way not even a modern submarine could match. How does he do it? We have some theories, but we won't know for certain until we can examine one alive and in working order. But what's even more interesting about the sperm whale is its tracking sonar—you've never heard anything like it."

After hearing Ken's description of the sound, I hope I never do, at least not at close range. "One hydrophone test," he said, "has indicated that the power of the signal is roughly equal to what you would encounter standing 20 feet directly behind a jet engine going at full blast!"

According to Ken, the sperm whale most likely makes the sound by clapping a pair of horny lips together, building the impulses up by rocketing them back and forth in a sort of echo chamber within its forehead, and finally emitting them in tiny, intensive bursts.

I asked what the whale does with the signal, and Ken shook his head.

"I can only give you a guess," he said. "I think he hunts with it, tracking one of his favorite foods, the giant squid. We suspect that the signal travels as far as 10 miles underwater, and that each sperm whale has his or her own 'signature'—that is, some small characteristic of the sound that distinguishes it from all other signals being broadcast. So if 'George' and 'Margaret' whale, let's say, are out hunting, 'George' pays attention only to his personal signal when it echoes back from a squid—and presumably he knows the squid's whereabouts and range by the direction and strength of the echo."

Only one thing troubled me. "How does he know it's a squid and not another sperm whale, or a shark?" I asked.

"If I knew all the answers," Ken said, grinning, "I wouldn't have to catch a live whale. Maybe when I do you can help me interview it."

We shook hands and I asked when he planned to start hunting, for I was on my way the next day to begin visiting Hawaii's other islands.

"We plan to do more research before we start," Ken answered. "But who knows? Maybe one day when you come back to Makapuu I'll introduce you to George or Margaret."

Wind and sea—elements of the seafaring heritage brought by the islands' early settlers—still challenge Hawaii's yachtsmen. Sailboats speed over the Pacific during the annual Labor Day race from Lahaina, Maui, to Honolulu.

Hawi

Mauna Kea

Kealakekua Bay

Mauna Loa

Hilo

Kilauea
Crater

Ka Lae
(South Cape)

HAWAII

Orchids, cattle, luxury resorts, and a restless goddess

LIKE MANY YOUNGSTERS—it is probably no more than half a million years old—it is larger and a trifle brasher than its elders. Someone has called it the "Texas of Hawaii," but that is misleading to outsiders. The island is less than half the size of Vermont.

Yet in a state where land is normally measured and valued by the square foot, the Island of Hawaii's 4,038 square miles have earned it the inevitable nickname, "Big Island"; it is nearly twice the size of its 131 smaller sisters put together. With a delightful blend of pride and self-effacing humor, Hawaii's 67,229 residents affectionately refer to the U. S. mainland as the "Big, *Big* Island."

It is an amiable giant, the Island of Hawaii, given only to occasional outbursts of temper—the fiery convulsions of its two currently active volcanoes, Mauna Loa and Kilauea. Yet even these are more youthful exhibition than murderous rampage: During prolonged eruptions, islanders, tourists, and scientists alike have stood in complete safety on an overlook at the crater rim of Kilauea Iki (Little Kilauea) while the world's mightiest blowtorch seared the sky to heights of 1,900 feet.

With deft hands, a picker gathers vanda orchids on Hawaii—the "Big Island"
—where orchids of every hue blossom on volcanic slopes. Growers export nearly
a million blooms a week to the mainland, the Far East, and to sister islands.

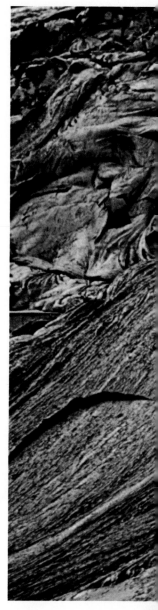

Overleaf: "Rolling her anger . . . In blood-red cataracts down to the sea!" As in Tennyson's "Kapiolani," the goddess Pele erupts from Kilauea Crater, December 30, 1969. A lava fountain jets as high as 1,600 feet; falling cinders strip trees.
NATIONAL PARK SERVICE PHOTO BY D. W. REESER

Only rarely has Kilauea trained its awesome weapons with seeming malice on man. In 1790 it wiped out a passing Hawaiian army with one monstrous exhalation of lethal gas. But as Gene Wilhelm points out, the army was asking for it—it had insulted Pele, goddess of volcanoes.

Gene is a former newspaperman and radio broadcaster who directs the Hawaii Visitors Bureau at Hilo, the Big Island's county seat and major city. Among many other things he advises visiting writers and photographers on the attractions of his island territory.

Time was when I almost thought Gene believed the old Hawaiian superstitions and fables he can quote by the score from memory. But now we are close friends, and I know he believes them. After three weeks of exploring his island I'm inclined to agree—there are things that can't be easily explained any other way. Take the business of the stones at Kohala that sang in the night until the people who borrowed them took them back where they belonged. But that is Phil Hooton's story and Phil comes a little later; it's best to wait and let him tell it himself.

Like any proper guest I began my tour of the Big Island with a personal call on its owner and guardian, the terrible-tempered goddess Pele, who gave Hawaii its second nickname, "Volcano Island." As it happened, I didn't see Pele, for she had just thrown a series of fiery tantrums at Kilauea and then retired into a chain of craters on the volcano's eastern slope. Dr. Powers thought she would probably sulk for some time.

As director of the U. S. Geological Survey's Hawaiian Volcano Observatory, in Hawaii Volcanoes National Park, Dr. Howard A. Powers is Madame Pele's resident analyst. Like many a counselor he puts up with such classic problems in his patient as sudden rages and withdrawals, long periods of moody silence, occasional threats, and running away from home.

"People tend to think of our volcanic eruptions as occurring over and over again in the exact same spot," Dr. Powers told me at his observatory office. We sat overlooking the immense fire pit of Halemaumau, or "fern house," a crater of the Kilauea complex named for nearby forests; hardly a fern or any other vegetation exists in the caldron itself.

"Hawaiian legend generally pictures Pele as a lady with restless feet," Dr. Powers continued, "and that's quite an accurate portrait." He indicated the bleak expanse of tortured stone far below us. "Since 1924 she has shown up in Halemaumau crater more than a dozen times, occasionally for a day or two but at least twice for visits of several months. Then she's off to stir things up in Kilauea Iki or in what we call the Chain of Craters, and after that very likely in an entirely separate volcano, Mauna Loa."

I asked about Hawaii's other giant, Mauna Kea, regarded as extinct.

"There's no such thing as a truly dead volcano," Dr. Powers answered. "After all, Hawaii has been building for quite some time, and there are volcanoes in these islands that erupted after silences of *three million years.* At the outside, Mauna Kea's last eruption took place only 11,000 years ago, and I expect Pele will pay it another visit in her own good time." He

Ranger probes a contorted lava landscape at Hawaii Volcanoes National Park, a preserve encompassing the island's two active volcanoes, Mauna Loa and Kilauea. At right, Dr. Howard A. Powers, head of the park volcano observatory, scans seismographs that record the tremors preceding eruptions. A geodimeter (left) measures stretching of a volcano's surface before an eruption.

smiled reassuringly. "But I wouldn't lie awake nights waiting for her."

Despite Pele's apparently aimless wanderings, she does show a long-term pattern of movement, beginning with Hawaii's oldest islands in the far northwest and building gradually southeastward to her youngest creation, Hawaii. I asked Dr. Powers if it were possible that she was at work on new surprises somewhere along the ocean floor beyond the Big Island.

"It's not only possible but likely," he answered. "In 1924 the bottom simply dropped out of Halemaumau; that is, the solid lava floor sank more than 1,500 feet. That means only one thing: The molten lava underneath had withdrawn in tremendous quantities. Well, where did it go? There was no corresponding eruption elsewhere on the island to siphon it off, and that leaves only one other possibility — a submarine vent.

"We have other evidence, too," he added, "in the form of countless small tremors showing on our seismographs as occurring to the southeast of us. And finally we have ocean soundings that record at least one submarine seamount several hundred miles from here along the line of the Hawaiian Ridge. It's highly symmetrical and therefore almost certainly volcanic. And we have underwater photographs showing fresh lava there."

He smiled. "I would say our wandering goddess isn't finished by any means. And neither is the State of Hawaii."

On my way out of the national park I stopped briefly at the site where a Hawaiian army paid a mortal price for snubbing Pele. Actually it was only part of an army and the snub was unintentional; a kinder deity than Pele might have overlooked it.

According to one version, the tragedy occurred during a march south from Hilo by an island chieftain, Keoua, to meet the army of his rival, Kamehameha I. Over the preceding weeks Keoua's 400 warriors had dutifully made offerings of fish to Pele, but the forced march ruled out normal courtesies. Divided into three groups, Keoua's army set out across the Kau Desert south of Kilauea. The second group never completed the march. Kilauea suddenly erupted, blanketing the area with sulphurous fumes and searing ash, instantly asphyxiating scores of warriors.

As quickly as the cloud came, it vanished; Keoua's third contingent found their comrades fallen in attitudes of attempted flight. Not long afterward rain turned the fine ash and sand of the desert to clay, temporarily preserving some of the footprints of one or both groups. Eventually the clay hardened into tuff and the memorial was complete, still to be seen today in an area of the park known as Footprints Trail.

Fortunately, Hawaii has more cheerful symbols than volcanoes and fossilized footprints. One of the symbols keeps Ann Kaya busy all week and incidentally gives Hawaii its third nickname, the "Orchid Island."

Ann manages a flower shop in Hilo called Ebesu's. Now and then for less than the price of a dozen roses on the mainland she air-ships to my home in Washington, D. C., a carton of what almost seems at first glance to be half the orchids in Hilo. Of course it isn't. Ann usually sends several stems with a dozen delicate blossoms on each one, while in an average week Hilo ships roughly one million orchids to the other islands, to the mainland, and to the Far East. No one knows exactly what Hilo earns for its trouble, but one side-benefit is the title "Orchid Capital of the World."

Guests in bold Hawaiian prints enjoy a luau at Kona Village, a remote resort on the Kona coast. Thatch-roof cabins face a timeless panorama: a sea-horizon nibbling at the setting sun. Fine beaches, excellent hunting and fishing, and scenic riding and hiking trails have drawn developers to the long-neglected coast.

Ironically, the same development that helped gain Hilo the distinction now threatens to turn part of the city into a horticultural wasteland. I learned of the problem from Milton Oda, the director of Hilo's largest wholesale shipper, Orchids of Hawaii. With a group of admiring tourists I had browsed through Mr. Oda's showroom, complete with free souvenir vanda orchids and gorgeous potted varieties on sale for as much as $35. Afterward Mr. Oda welcomed me to his office to discuss the technique of growing and selling some 30 million orchids a year.

"Growing is no great problem so long as you have an expert staff," Mr. Oda explained. "As you know, orchids are air plants requiring very little soil, and with a proper start they take quite good care of themselves. Transportation was always the great hurdle to overseas business, and now the jet has solved that — we have several planeloads a week leaving Hilo's new international airport, along with shipments on dozens of passenger jets flying directly to the mainland." He looked grave. "But the price is very high."

I was surprised, for with new competition on the transpacific route I had understood that air-cargo rates were actually being lowered.

"I do not mean money," Mr. Oda said. "The price is to the orchids themselves, in terms of jet exhaust and pollution. We used to have most of our nurseries in the Hilo area, but the orchids cannot stand it any longer. Oh, they survive, and perhaps the average customer would not notice the damage. But *I* can see it, in the faded colors and other imperfections, and I will not sell orchids of such quality. We have bought land 25 miles southeast of here, where our flowers can breathe pure air once more."

The same quiet atmosphere and pure air of Hawaii appeal to Laurance S. Rockefeller. In the early 1960's the prominent financier and conservationist chose the Big Island for what today is a model among resort developments throughout the 50th State — Mauna Kea Beach Hotel. The $21,000,000 retreat lies on the leeward side of the Big Island near Kawaihae Bay, whose name means literally "water of wrath," after a nearby fresh pool so well situated that early Hawaiians fought over it.

Today a more genteel struggle characterizes Kawaihae, in the form of competition for rooms at Mauna Kea Beach. Despite heavy bookings the hotel's likable manager, Bob Butterfield, said he had space for me for two days and a night.

Unlike many a resort hotel in the islands, Mauna Kea Beach follows my friend David Kaapu's principle of mauka-makai, fitting unobtrusively into the contours of the coastal hills so as not to block the view of tranquil Kawaihae Bay from farther inland. It follows other principles characteristic of Rockefeller design: open courtyards and balconies providing an air of quiet spaciousness; generously proportioned and equipped rooms; furnishings that in many cases amount to artistic treasures; and the blend of privacy and community life that distinguishes great hotels.

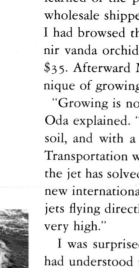

Prize-winning Pacific blue marlin tips the scales at 724 pounds at Kailua pier during the 1969 Hawaiian International Billfish Tournament. Above, anglers beseech a big one to take their line. Sport fishermen, largely unrestricted by seasons, limits, or license requirements, troll for tuna, marlin, and dolphin.

One thing Mauna Kea Beach is not—a place for round-the-clock revelry. Mr. Rockefeller thinks of it in terms of the quiet relaxation that many seek in a Hawaiian vacation but don't always find. "Leaders from many walks of life," he says simply, "are the forgotten people—society tends to forget they're human too. They must be revitalized. This is the kind of place they can come to for that."

I have never considered myself in the category of a leader, but I nonetheless enjoyed Mr. Rockefeller's hotel, especially his electric toasters. Mauna Kea Beach is the only place I have encountered where every room-service breakfast order comes with its own individual toaster, so that the results will be exactly to a guest's liking.

At least one attractive development on the Big Island had its origin in a major disaster. Though Hilo has the look of a city that could do with a little refurbishing here and there, it has a magnificently open waterfront park that is the envy of almost every port community in the state. The way Hilo got it is the envy of no one.

The wave was born thousands of miles to the southeast of Hawaii, off the coast of Chile during the early hours of May 22, 1960. By a combination of factors long known to science but still not entirely understood, a submarine earthquake generated the wave and sent it streaking silently across the Pacific.

Seismic sea waves—or tsunamis, as they are often called—are neither tidal waves nor ordinary ocean swells. They are a series of almost invisible waves that travel at speeds exceeding 600 miles an hour in very deep water and are detectable at sea only by sensitive shore-based instruments. As they approach land, however, tsunamis exchange invisibility and speed for terrifying mass and destructive power capable of removing anything in the way.

As had happened before, Hilo was in the way.

"It was not only in the way, but highly vulnerable," says Capt. Robert C. Munson, director of the U. S. Coast and Geodetic Survey's Honolulu Field Office in the State of Hawaii and its Seismic Sea-Wave Warning System. Before visiting the Big Island I had heard of the 1960 wave and had called on Captain Munson at the control center in Ewa Beach, just west of Honolulu. With a huge wall map of the Pacific area he gave me a brief course on tsunamis.

Kailua villager harvests ripe coffee cherries, cultivated by Japanese on tiny island farms since the 1930's.

"As a rule," he began, "seismic sea waves in Hawaii come from one of three directions: the general area of Japan to the northwest, Alaska to the north, or from Chile and Peru to the southeast. These regions occasionally have the type of earthquakes that generate tsunamis." He swept a hand along the northwestern part of the Hawaiian archipelago.

"Right there, you're looking at one of the world's longest and finest natural breakwaters. When a tsunami comes in from the northwest, those relatively uninhabited islands of Kure, Midway, and others down the line actually *split* the force of the wave and deflect it from the populated islands of Kauai, Oahu, Maui, and the others." He ran a finger in the opposite direction, beginning on the west coast of South America and crossing the region of virtually empty ocean to the Island of Hawaii. "But here, there isn't any breakwater.

"In addition," Captain Munson said, "Hilo Bay is funnel-shaped, and so it amplifies the effect of a tsunami. No amount of warning in 1960 could have saved the city completely."

In the end the warning helped, although some people in Hilo made a fatal miscalculation. As the wave spread across the southeastern Pacific, reports from various remote islands indicated a rise in water level of no more than a foot. Finally, from South Cape on the Big Island itself, came word of a two-foot rise. With that, against all advice of the Seismic Sea-Wave Warning System, a handful of people in Hilo went down to see the wave come in shortly after midnight.

It came in 35 feet high.

"Afterward," says Gene Wilhelm, "people here took to calling it Hilo's instant urban-renewal program. It was more a case of urban *removal,* to the extent of $25,000,000 and 61 lives—many of the people who went down to see the wave were killed. Fortunately, Hilo is built mostly on high ground. The waterfront took virtually the full blow, in a strip about 300 yards wide along the shore.

"I slept through the night the waves struck," Gene continued, "but the next morning I talked with witnesses, and wrote the lead story for our *Hilo Tribune-Herald.* The waterfront was unrecognizable. There were several waves, you see, and what the first didn't get the others took care of. Whole buildings were driven directly through the ones behind, the way you'd close a telescope. Boulders weighing nearly a ton were picked up and set down hundreds of yards away. And through it all there was the sickening thunder of buildings disintegrating, with the screams of people trapped inside."

An acquaintance of Gene's, an electrical-company supervisor named Shigeto Matsubara, was among the lucky ones who escaped from the waterfront unharmed. He had been checking a power station in the harbor area and had delayed a moment too long in getting out. As he left the station, the wave swept silently in and plucked him off his feet.

Raker ensures the even sun-drying of Kona coffee beans, once popular in blends but now dwindling as an export.

"It didn't crest or roar like other big waves," Mr. Matsubara told me in recalling the experience. "I can only describe it as a sudden *presence* of water. And there we were, the wave and I, riding up one of the main streets with buildings going down on either side and with me floating upright high off the ground, like a maharaja on his elephant."

Miraculously, the wave ran its course and set Mr. Matsubara down so lightly on his feet that he simply walked—or rather, raced—out of reach of the succeeding waves. I asked if he had been injured in any way.

"Not by the wave," he answered. "But I must have given such a terrible shout when it picked me up that I paralyzed my vocal cords, because for three months afterward I didn't have any voice."

The legendary figure of that night in Hilo is Mrs. Fusayo Ito, who was 50 at the time and who put to sea involuntarily aboard an oversized window screen. She had been standing inside the door of her house near the waterfront, uncertain of what to do, when the wave struck and decided for her. Battering in the door, it scooped her up and washed her back and forth between the street and her hallway several times. On the final round trip she managed to clutch a heavy wood-framed screen. Then she was off on the wave's giant backwash into the harbor.

It was a voyage Mrs. Ito is not likely to forget. Once in the harbor she found herself surrounded by such a solid mass of debris that she considered clambering back across it to shore. Then she changed her mind and decided to float on in hope of rescue. The water grew cold and she gathered passing bunches of grass, wrapping them around her feet for insulation. The rest of the time she spent avoiding heavy debris, such as logs and building timbers.

Friends later asked Mrs. Ito why she hadn't transferred to something more substantial than her window screen, and it was here that she revealed an instinct for seamanship. She answered that she had preferred maneuverability to sheer mass, and that she had worked out a system of navigating with the screen.

"It barely floated," she explained, "so I did not lie full on it, but only half-way, with the rest of me in the water. Whenever I saw a big log coming at me in the gloom, I would take a breath, put my full weight on the screen, and we would dive underneath and come up on the other side."

All night long Mrs. Ito maneuvered with her screen, alternately diving and surfacing to avoid collisions. And every spare moment she prayed that someone would find her. In the early morning of May 23, six hours after the wave had seized her, rescuers picked her up three miles offshore.

She rather regrets that they didn't salvage the screen.

While the Big Island keeps a vigilant watch on the sea, it maintains an equally keen one into the far reaches of the sky. One morning with Gene Wilhelm I rode in a four-wheel-drive station wagon up a winding cinder trail to the summit of Mauna Kea volcano, 40 miles overland from Hilo. Here on the crater rim at 13,796 feet the University of Hawaii was building the world's highest astronomical observatory, with a giant new 88-inch reflecting telescope.

At close range Mauna Kea has the look of some cosmic slag heap, a monstrous scrap pile of leftovers from creation. Among the scorched and rusting shapes of giant cinder cones on the upper slope we passed through endless stretches of volcanic debris, varying in size from the

Smiling parishioner pauses outside St. Benedict's Church in the hamlet of Honaunau. Inside, murals of Biblical scenes, painted about 1900, decorate the walls. Beneath waving palms, Father Ralph W. Sylva baptizes an infant.

finest gravel to boulders as big as railroad cars. In the early-morning sun the mountain seemed almost incandescent, a great mass of fiery red tones mixed with vivid yellows and oranges, streaked here and there by the volcano's own dark breath.

Despite its infernal appearance Mauna Kea can be bitterly cold, and above 9,000 feet I was glad of a heavy parka. At the very top the volcano lives up to its name, "white mountain," for there is snow in pockets and crevices all year round. "It sounds odd for a tropical paradise," Gene said, "but Hawaii is one of those places where people can, and do, ski several months out of the year."

Personally, I would rather do my skiing somewhere else, for even the mildest exercise atop Mauna Kea can be exhausting. Inside the observatory we met Norman Crapo, a veteran supervisor on high-altitude construction jobs. Under direction of the Stewart-Berg Corporation of Seattle, Washington, he and his 18-man crew were putting the final touches on the observatory building before installing the telescope.

Norm and I fell to discussing the effects of Mauna Kea's rarefied atmosphere on the human body. I had heard of people in Hilo who declined invitations to visit the observatory for fear of a heart attack or other complications.

"That's overdoing it a little," Norm said smiling, "but it's true the lack of oxygen puts a strain on you. After a while you tend to adjust, but at best our average man here operates at no more than 35 to 40 percent efficiency. And our average man is something special," he added. "Despite high pay, only one out of ten workers who start on the job stays longer than a month."

I asked what the more noticeable effects of the altitude were, and Norm said simply, "Get down on the floor and do five fast push-ups for me, then spell 'Seattle.'"

I managed all five and he gave me a hand up. Feeling dizzy but quite pleased with myself, I fumbled and started to spell Seattle with a "C."

"It's a matter of air pressure," Norm explained when my dizziness had passed. "At sea level, air pressure is 14.7 pounds per square inch, but up here it's only around nine, so that with every breath you get roughly three-fifths the normal amount of oxygen. When you exert yourself and need even more oxygen, your brain gets a little starved and woozy.

"It's bad enough for construction workers," he continued, "but it would never do for astronomers. Among other things, the University of Hawaii people are going to run planetary studies for future U. S. space shots. That's a pretty complicated business and it calls for absolute precision. So the observatory is designed to be more or less airtight, with its own special atmosphere enriched to 28 percent oxygen." He grinned. "Breathing that stuff, you could spell any word in the dictionary."

It was autumn roundup time when I reached Richard Smart's ranch, so I only stopped for a cup of coffee with him. Following the coast road from Hilo I had driven around the northern flank of Mauna Kea to ranch headquarters at the small town of Waimea. The U. S. Post Office, in despair over the number of other Waimeas in the 50th State, refers to the town as Kamuela, a practice regarded as outrageous by some old-timers.

Products of the woodcarver's art, Polynesian gods grimace, outrigger canoes wait as if to sail legendary seas, plump birds roost, and a whale swims overhead in the Hawi studio of Phil Hooton. An expert on early Polynesian art and culture, Mr. Hooton wields knives and chisels to help preserve Hawaii's artistic heritage. Here he carefully fits a limpet shell lid on a jewelry box.

Mr. Smart's ranch is the gigantic Parker spread, often described as the country's largest singly owned cattle range. I asked Mr. Smart, a successful actor turned highly successful rancher, if the description was accurate.

"It may have been once," he answered. "The famous King Ranch in Texas is a corporation, whereas this spread has always belonged entirely to my mother's family, the Parkers, beginning with an original grant from Kamehameha III. But I think there is a private ranch now in the New Mexico-Arizona area that runs more than our 220,000 acres. As far as other countries go, there are ranches in Australia where you could probably drop this one and never find it again."

With some 47,000 head of Hereford cattle, Parker supplies roughly 20 percent of all beef consumed in the islands, a massive undertaking. In recent years, however, the ranch has sold or leased some of its vast acreage for developments such as Laurance Rockefeller's Mauna Kea Beach. I asked Mr. Smart if he envisioned a gradual shift away from cattle into real estate.

"Not if I can help it," he answered decisively. "I believe in development, but not at the expense of ranching, sugarcane, and pineapple, not to mention pure uncluttered space. Our salvation in the islands lies in combining all those elements in proportion, not in blanketing this area with one and that area with another. We have introduced people to Parker land, but it still is — and I hope always will be — cattle country, too."

Certainly Kamehameha I, grandfather of the man responsible for the Parker deed, would have approved of Richard Smart's philosophy. He came from the wide and beautiful region north of the ranch, and he was known as the "Lonely One."

He was lonely in the sense of being a towering figure among his people, a man removed from other men by his great energy and enormous vision. He was unquestionably the father of the Hawaiian nation, yet a stranger to many of the gentler qualities that distinguish it. He was proud, ruthless, shrewd often to the point of cunning, rarely given to doubt or indecision, and utterly devoted to the Hawaiian people. Largely against their will he forced them to lay aside old differences and to unite under single rule, foreseeing a time when they would not survive without common strength and purpose in the face of advancing Western influence.

Having succeeded, Kamehameha the Great died in 1819 at Kailua on the Big Island and was buried in secrecy lest his enemies find his bones and derive supernatural power from them. As a result, no one knows the whereabouts of his grave. His monument is the State of Hawaii.

Like its famous son, the Kohala District on the northern tip of the Big Island has an air of lonely majesty. It is a sparsely peopled land and one that is rarely still, for it is the home of Apaapaa, the powerful ocean

Browsing in Neptune's attic, diver Jim Robinson pursues a hobby: collecting antique bottles like those above, dropped overboard through the years from sailing ships in Kailua Bay. Two more lie beside the encrusted fluke of a lost anchor.

breeze. I came to it across rolling hills of sugarcane and tall pasture flecked with sunlight and endlessly furrowed in shifting patterns by the wind. Under the lash of Apaapaa, the region's few trees take on human shapes, bowing almost to the ground as though forever harvesting the gold and emerald fields.

Such a land appeals to the eye and instinct of men like Phil Hooton, an unsurpassed genius in the traditional art of Polynesian wood sculpture. Phil's creations seldom appear in shops, for they are usually commissioned or quickly spoken for by dealers and museums. More often than not it takes an expert to distinguish between one of Phil's copies of an ancient masterwork and the original itself.

Friends in Hilo had told me about Phil and I called at his studio in the remote village of Hawi, on a steep hillside overlooking the sea. I found him and his attractive wife Barbara amid a clutter of wonderfully graceful and intricately carved figures—slender dolphins, or *mahimahi,* in the act of leaping the waves; grimacing miniatures of Polynesian gods; birds in flight so realistic that one could almost hear the whisper of their wings; and a superb model of a *kaulua,* or double-hulled canoe, that on a larger scale might well have brought the early discoverers to Hawaii. I was pleased to note that in Phil's sizable reference library there were several copies of the NATIONAL GEOGRAPHIC, as well as one of the Society's Special Publications, *Isles of the South Pacific.*

Few authorities today can match Phil Hooton's knowledge of Polynesian art and the culture that nurtured it. I asked what he thought its chances of survival were under the impact of Western civilization.

"Probably small, except in minor ways," he answered. "Too many of the people who claim to preserve Polynesian culture are what I would call 'professional Polynesians,' those who are interested primarily in the market and what it demands, whether it's valid or not. For example, it's rare today in the islands that you find authentic Polynesian dance—or hula, if you prefer. The classic forms have been so altered and popularized that most audiences won't stand for the real thing. They think it's poor hula because it's not what they've been led to expect.

"As for the real authorities," Phil continued, "too often they bicker over minute details of Polynesian culture, insisting that this or that aspect of it was the *true* one. But that's like arguing over whether the early New Englander or the Southerner was the real American—they had different customs, different architecture, different foods, and even different accents, but essentially they were products of the same civilization."

Turning the subject around, I asked Phil what he thought would survive from the culture of ancient Polynesia. He pondered a moment and then said with a faint smile, "Some of the old legends and beliefs. Take the charter fishermen at Kailua in the Kona District, on the coast south of here. They're practical men with not a bit of nonsense to them, and they know their business inside out. Most of them are haole, without a drop of Hawaiian blood in them, and they're not a superstitious lot. But it's the rare one who's never tied a bunch of ti leaves to his wheelhouse roof before heading out for the big *a'u*—the marlin. Any true Hawaiian can tell you the ti leaf holds special powers for the sailor, just

Minerals paint sands of Hawaiian beaches in subtle tones: Crystals of olivine tint a beach green near South Cape (above). Obsidian darkens Black Sand Beach (left), and fragments of shell and coral whiten a strand on the Kona coast.

Long-stemmed anthuriums tipped with waxy blossoms brighten a nursery near Mountain View. Slow to mature, the plants require a year and a half to begin producing marketable flowers. Island growers sell more Anthurium andraeanum *than any other bloom; delicate vanda orchids rank second, carnations third.*

as he can tell you bananas aboard a boat mean almost certain trouble."

"Don't think we're making fun of superstition," Barbara added, pointing to a very ordinary looking strip of wood over the studio doorway. "That's a piece from the *kauila* tree, and it wards off evil spirits. Phil feels happier with it there, and so do I."

I glanced at Phil and he nodded. "Say what you like," he remarked, "but there are things about the ancient beliefs and traditions that can't be explained in a scientific way. Not long ago there was a family in the Kohala District that took some stones from an old *heiau*, or Hawaiian shrine, to use as flagstones for their front path. That was just fine, but then the stones began to sing at night—a sort of high, plaintive wail that kept everybody in the house awake. Finally, the family took the stones back to the heiau so they could get a decent night's sleep."

I couldn't help feeling slightly skeptical, and I asked Phil if he believed the story himself.

"Let's put it this way," he answered with a disarming grin. "If I needed a few flagstones for my front path I'd think twice about raiding a heiau —then I'd go and get them somewhere else."

So would any ancient Hawaiian who valued his life, for heiaus were once protected by kapus so rigid that only the most foolhardy dared violate them. Nor would that long-ago islander have considered eating in the company of women, or allowing his wife to taste pork, bananas, coconuts, turtle, or certain kinds of fish. He would as soon have built a canoe without first asking the tree's permission to cut it down, or have let his shadow fall on a king or an *ali'i*, a lesser chief. For any one of those sins, plus a variety of others, he would have paid the standard price—a sacrificial club to the head.

Unless, of course, he could escape to Honaunau.

Honaunau lies some 55 miles south along the coast, near the sport-fishing center and thriving resort town of Kailua, one of the Big Island's most rapidly developing areas. By contrast, Honaunau is a quiet village whose main attraction is its City of Refuge, a historic monument recently restored and now managed by the U. S. National Park Service.

In fact, Honaunau's "city" was never a city at all in the sense of a permanent dwelling place for large numbers of people. With the exception of a few *kahunas*, or priests, the population was strictly transient, an endless cycle of fugitives seeking pardon for violation of the kapus or for simply choosing the wrong side in a war.

"Honaunau was sort of a poor man's answer to the kapu," says Tom Vaughan, the monument's gifted and very likable archeologist. Tom had given me a tour of the park's major points, including an area adjoining the sanctuary proper, where the king of the district had lived with his court. The sanctuary itself was simply a barren promontory thrusting out to sea, with its landward side barricaded by a 12-foot-high wall of expertly fitted lava rocks.

"The old Hawaiian social system," Tom explained, "was basically feudal, with rigid class distinctions reflected by the kapus. What they added up to was a pyramid of privilege, with a king at the top who could do almost no wrong and a common man at the bottom who could do a lot of it.

Sale day at Parker Ranch: Stolid Hereford bull faces buyers during the annual Hawaii Cattlemen's Association Bull and Horse Sale. Women at right follow the proceedings from seats up front. The sleek champion above bears faint resemblance to the scrawny Mexican longhorns English explorer George Vancouver introduced to the islands in 1793. Protected by a strict 10-year kapu so they could multiply in safety, the cattle soon numbered in thousands. In 1847 John Palmer Parker, great-great-great-grandfather of today's owner of the Parker Ranch, began domesticating the cattle and selling beef to whalers. Parker's descendants built the spread into one of the Nation's largest privately owned ranches. Some 47,000 cattle graze its 220,000 acres; 600 miles of fences contain them.

"It would have been an intolerable system without some sort of loop-holes for the common man," Tom continued. "Honaunau and a few places like it were the loopholes." He swept his hand toward the giant barrier of lava rocks towering above us.

"No matter who you were or what you had done, if you could reach the other side of that wall by land or sea you were safe. The beauty of it was that you didn't have to stay there. Once the priests had absolved you, usually within a day, you were free to walk out—and all the kings in Hawaii couldn't touch you. If you were a refugee from war, you simply waited for peace, and you had the same immunity from your enemies."

As always, the road to salvation had its pitfalls. To reach the refuge from the landward side a fugitive had to run the blockade of the king's entire household, with its additional gauntlet of royal troops. Here the odds were heavy, and to a seafaring people the best hope often seemed an approach by water.

"For a Hawaiian it wasn't all that much of a swim," Tom said, indicating another spit of land several hundred yards to the north of the refuge and separated from it by a deep bay. "If you could make it overland to a point along that shore, you had half the battle won—but the last stretch had its gauntlet, too. You can barely make it out, a patch of dark water in the bay. The Hawaiians call it Lua Mano."

The term was vaguely familiar, but I couldn't place it.

"It means 'den of the shark,' " said Tom.

I thought of Lua Mano a day or so later, on my way to visit the monu-ment to Captain Cook. The great English navigator and discoverer of Hawaii had met death in a skirmish with the natives at Kealakekua Bay, just north of the City of Refuge.

The tragedy occurred on February 14, 1779, and Cook's shipmates—including his sailing master, William Bligh, later captain of His Majesty's Armed Vessel *Bounty*—failed to recover all of their leader's remains. With their belief in the supernatural power of human bones, especially those of a great chief, the Hawaiians had dismembered Cook's body shortly after the battle and were able to produce only some of the bones during a later reconciliation with the ship's crew. These the British buried with naval honors in the bay; a century later his country raised a mon-ument on shore to Cook's memory. By coincidence, the man who takes care of the monument today is part British.

You would never know it to look at him, for at 52 Henry Leslie is the nearly perfect image of a Hawaiian—dark of skin, classic in feature, gentle of manner, and blessed with a dazzling smile. Only a wiry build sets Henry off from the pure Hawaiian, who generally runs to more massive proportions.

I met Henry in the village of Napoopoo, where I had gone in hope of hiring a boat to visit Cook's monument, two miles north along a sheer rampart of coastal cliffs. Sightseeing boats out of Kailua make the trip daily, but they don't touch shore. Also I had heard of Henry's part-time job as caretaker of the monument and I had hoped to meet him as well.

I reached Napoopoo early in the morning, but not early enough—the fishermen had long since departed for their offshore grounds. The only

Mounted hunter, carcass of wild pig slung across his saddle, fords a stream in the Waipio Valley, a scenic gash in the green mountains of Hawaii's northern coast. In 1946 a tsunami — seismic sea wave — roared inland and swept the fertile valley clean of taro farms and homes, but left undisturbed its primeval grandeur.

thing that had kept Henry behind was a broken clutch on his boat. He apologized for not being able to show me the monument personally.

Instead we talked about how Henry got the job and of some of his experiences over the years. He told me that the British Consul in Honolulu had hired him in 1959 to keep an eye on the monument—a plain, 10-foot-high granite obelisk set in a small plot of grass at the water's edge. Henry visits the site once every week or 10 days to cut and weed the grass and to pick up after occasional visitors from private boats. I asked if the British Consul also paid him, and Henry shook his head.

"The British Admiralty pays me," he said with a touch of pride. "Every three months they send me a check all the way from London, right here to Napoopoo. It's made out in pounds, but I have friends in a Kailua bank and they give me dollars for it. The Admiralty's very careful about records and things; I always sign the receipt and send it back."

Only once since he was hired have Henry's employers shown uneasiness about the monument, and that was when it disappeared for a week.

"I don't blame them," Henry said, obviously grieved by the memory, "but I love that monument, too, and I would never let anybody steal it. It was there all the time, behind the painting."

The episode had begun when a film company from California arrived to make a documentary of Cook's exploits in Hawaii. They asked Henry's permission to work on location beside the beach at Kealakekua Bay, and he agreed so long as they didn't disturb anything.

"But of course," as he explained to me, "you couldn't have some actor playing Captain Cook walking up and down the beach in front of his own memorial. The movie people asked me if they could put a painting up in front of it—you know, with trees and things to match the background. I said all right, but don't hurt the monument." He shook his head in admiration. "That was some beautiful painting."

Too beautiful, in fact. A day or so later passengers aboard a sightseeing boat from Kailua spied people walking up and down the beach with a lot of equipment—and no monument. Somehow word got back to the British Consul in Honolulu, and he put in a call to Henry.

The first 30 seconds of the call are not ones that Henry looks back on fondly, for he had trouble getting a word in edgewise.

"Finally, I managed to explain," he told me, "and the Consul was very nice about it. In fact, he was pleased that somebody was making a movie about Captain Cook, and he hoped he would get a chance to see it. I don't know if he ever did, though."

The account made me even more eager to see the monument myself. But I was leaving the next morning for the Island of Maui, and I was too late that day to catch the sightseeing boat out of Kailua. I asked Henry if I could reach the monument on foot from Napoopoo.

"Yes," he answered after a pause. "It's a little rough going, because the base of the cliff is covered with boulders from all the slides, and there are

In a tidal-pool tub, a girl of Milolii bathes her sister. Long a remote fishing settlement on Hawaii's windswept west coast, Milolii now anchors one end of a new highway, a development that inevitably dooms its simple existence.

Men and women of Milolii preside over the last days of a dying era. Women at right slice tuna for a luau celebrating completion of the new highway. Visitors to the town will still see fishermen pulling canoes ashore (opposite, above) and hanging out russet nets to dry on a beach littered with coral chunks (above), but already changes have come. Once Milolii fishermen cut koa trees for their canoes; now they buy plywood. They must truck their catch to Hilo, 95 miles away, and freight charges make fishing barely profitable. More and more young people seek jobs in the cities. Now, with tourists visiting, Miloliians see more of the things their small incomes will not buy, and frustration hastens the disintegration of their unhurried and easygoing culture.

one or two spots where you have to swim a few yards. But you shouldn't have any trouble."

After some weeks in Hawaii I had learned the wisdom of carrying swimming trunks in the car at all times. With these and some old sneakers I set out on the round trip of a little less than four miles.

Even with an edge of some ten years on Henry, I am plainly not as agile as he is. I found the boulders very rough going and I can't recall a single level square foot in the whole four miles. And the swimming was something else again.

At the first point, where a sheer wall of rock barred the way, I slipped into the water and discovered, as I should have foreseen, that the cliff continued just as sheerly underwater; there was no hope of wading even part of the way. What was worse, I found myself caught in a heavy surge along the cliff, a great rhythmic thrust of water that carried me eight or ten feet up the face of the rock so that I skimmed it by inches. Each time on the backwash the surge swept me twenty feet or more out to sea.

At such times I have an unfailing talent for disagreeable thoughts and I suddenly recalled Lua Mano, the den of the shark. My situation was uncomfortable and I could only hope any passing shark would concur — and steer a little farther out to sea.

In the end the surge proved less dangerous than it looked, and I simply stroked away, alternately climbing the cliff and sliding seaward, but making progress toward the goal. After further hiking ashore, and one or two more rides on the marine roller coaster, I reached the monument.

There was a simple dignity to it befitting a man of Cook's character, and one detail that I'm sure would have delighted him. Henry had told me that every year or so a warship from one of the British Commonwealth countries pays a call at the monument, sending a landing party ashore to make any necessary repairs to the stone foundation and to the chain railing around the obelisk.

On a concrete walkway leading from the monument toward the water, I found that each ship had imbedded its colorful metal or enamel seal in the pavement, as a memento of its visit. There were few dates, but from the bleached and faded colors of some of the seals, they obviously stretched back many years. Nor could an American tell what kinds of ships they had been, with such names as *St. Croix, Beacon Hill, Jonquière,* and *Sussexvale.* One could say of them only that they had followed in the wake of one of history's great explorers and of a sister ship well named — H.M.S. *Resolution.*

Henry was gone when I returned to Napoopoo, probably to town to look for a new clutch. I didn't see him again, but I had a final glimpse of the monument as I flew out of Kailua early the next morning. Then the plane swung away and we were headed north for a neighboring island with the name of another great seafarer, the one called Maui.

He was a rogue, a demigod, and a fisherman all in one, and he hauled the islands of the Pacific up from the depths with his line. Then he gave the prettiest one his name, or so say the people on Maui. They put it another way: *Maui no ka oi* — "Maui is best." Of course that's a slight exaggeration, as Hawaiians readily admit. All but the 42,226 on Maui.

Akaka Falls drops a silver plume 420 feet over a volcanic cliff near Honomu. Riotous tropical vegetation feeds on frequent showers and the fall's ceaseless spray. Twisted aerial roots climb skyward and ti plants sprout flaming leaves.

Lahaina

Puu Kukui +

• Wailuku

Haleakala Crater

• Hana

MAUI

Busy farms, a port with a past, a village near heaven

TO BEGIN WITH, they are a little like Maui himself—clever, energetic, and quick to laugh. But Maui was a spirit, a heartless one at that, and they are as warm as any people can be.

Their home is actually two islands in one, a pair of volcanic Siamese twins somewhat uneven in size. The enormous peaks are fused together by a low-lying isthmus that gives Maui its nickname, the "Valley Island." Like most twins the two regions are entirely different in character: West Maui, the extrovert and bustling tourist center; East Maui, the serene child of nature. Like many twins, too, they are good-natured rivals—among the people of East Maui the rest of the island is known somewhat loftily as the "Other Side."

One can excuse the loftiness on poetic grounds, for Maui's easternmost community, the quiet village of Hana, is said to be only a step or two from heaven. When it rains in Hana, goes an old Hawaiian song, it rains *Lani, ha'a, ha'a* — "Heaven, step, step" — almost no distance at all. Hana's space-minded children have seized on the legend to suggest that the United States transfer its Apollo launching facility from Cape Kennedy

Dwarfed by a frothy breaker, a surfer rides toward the foam-laced shore of Maui. This second largest of the Hawaiian Islands bears the name of a roguish demigod who, legends say, pulled it from the ocean floor with his fishhook.

GORDON W. GAHAN

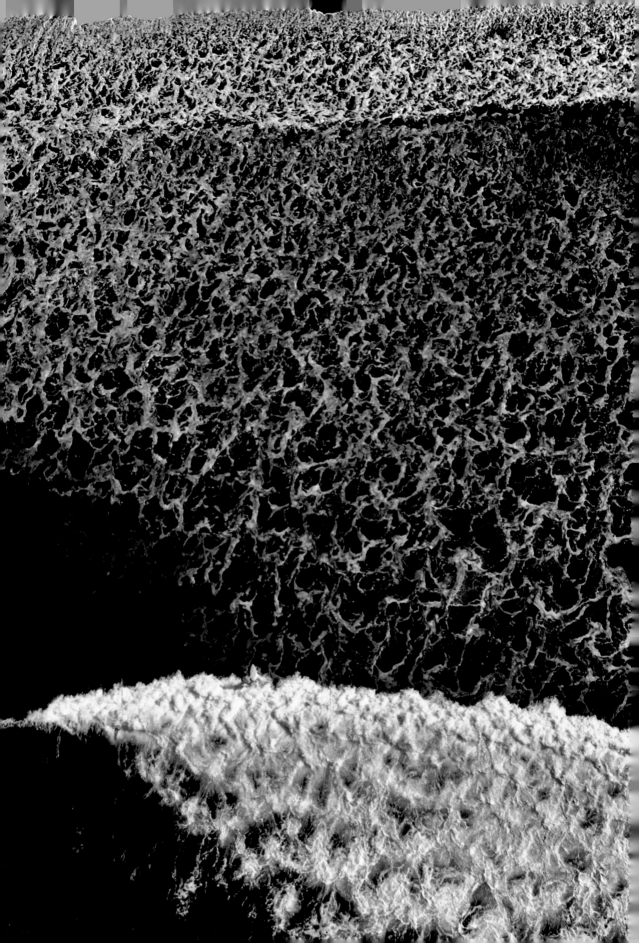

Overleaf: Like volcanoes in miniature, cinder cones pock Haleakala Crater. Eons of erosion shaped the 2.5-by-7.5-mile depression. Later eruptions cluttered its floor with volcanic debris. Now dormant, Haleakala last erupted about 1790; two minor flows, far down its slopes, reached the sea, altering Maui's coastline.

to their school playground, since it is practically next door to the moon!

It is a generous offer, but I'm personally against it. For one thing it might mean the end of *Ho'olaule'a o Hana* as I remember it, and there aren't many such things left in Hawaii.

Ho'olaule'a o Hana, or "Festival of Hana," is a week-long celebration held every autumn by the village's 300 residents. Unlike the corresponding "Aloha Week" in many a larger city, Hana's festival has none of the overtones of a commercial tourist attraction; it is strictly a hometown affair. Fortunately, however, visitors are more than welcome, and Joe Daniels invited me to join in.

Joe is part Hawaiian, part Danish, and part Chinese and he works as a supervisor for Hana Ranch, the largest employer in East Maui. The company also owns the superb Hotel Hana Ranch, and Joe helps out there as a director of guest activities. In addition he is personal adviser and friend seemingly to the entire younger generation of Hana, a role that keeps him hopping during festival week.

I arrived in town on Saturday afternoon, just in time for the riding exhibitions. A good many of Hana's men are paniolos—cowboys. The Hawaiian term is a corruption of *espagñoles* and dates back to the days when most ranch hands in the islands were Mexican immigrants, and thus considered Spanish.

The riding exhibition was strictly for youngsters, who proved hardly less skillful than their fathers. I had expected something on the order of a rodeo, but Joe explained that this was a more formal occasion.

"We have plenty of rodeos," he said, "and they're pretty lively affairs, but once a year Hana likes to put on its finery and ride as if it had never heard of a range cow."

The finery was impressive, with horsemanship to match. As we took our places around the school playground some 30 or 40 students, boys and girls from the junior and senior high schools, appeared on horseback, paired off and dressed in dazzling silk costumes. Each couple wore the symbolic color of one of Hawaii's eight major islands—pink for Maui, orange-yellow for Oahu, red for the Big Island, and so on. In addition, each girl wore a crown woven of her island's official flower, such as Maui's *loke-lani*, or "heavenly rose."

In well-coordinated lines the riders traced patterns across the field, first at a trot and then at a canter. I was amazed that children brought up on cow ponies could display such classic riding-school form. For a finale they passed in review by couples before the judges, again at a trot, at a canter, and then at a gallop.

With fine impartiality the judges awarded first prize to a couple in the misty gray color of Niihau Island, bestowing second and third honors on couples representing Oahu and Maui respectively. Other prizes were awarded for parade floats built the previous week by various school

Inside the "house of the sun" riders cross Haleakala Crater, where the demigod Maui snared the sun. Frank Freitas (below) guides mortals through this home of the rare silversword (below, left). Shiny hairs on its leaves reflect sunlight, conserving moisture. A relative of the sunflower, it blooms once, then dies.

grades, and then everybody went home to rest up for Sunday afternoon.

If the horse show seemed sedate, Hana more than made up for it next day in the athletic games and competitions. The principle was the same as that of the old-fashioned New England town fair, but the events were strictly out of Hana's Polynesian way of life. There were contests in coconut husking; casting the *'upena kiloi,* or throwing net; racing in giant wooden clogs fitted with footholds for teams of six contestants to a pair; bowling, or *'ulu maika,* using the traditional Hawaiian stones shaped like hockey pucks; and finally that universal test of strength combined with sheer bulk, the tug-of-war.

It was here that the Hawaiian physique came into its own, for islanders with relatively pure Polynesian blood frequently run to giant dimensions. The tug-of-war rules limited each women's team to a total of 1,000 pounds, a restriction explained to me with many a giggle by one small girl: "It means no more than three ladies on a side."

Actually, the number was six, but Hana's women nonetheless demonstrated considerable brawn. In the men's event the number of contestants was the same, but the weight went up 600 pounds, with a result suggestive of bulldozers straining in opposite directions. As it was, I suspect that whoever provided the manila rope for the competition got it back a fathom or two longer.

The day ended long after sunset with a concert by Hana's amateur choral group under the direction of a lady of genius, Mrs. Martha Hohu. She comes down once a week from Honolulu's Bernice P. Bishop Museum to train Hana in the music of its forebears.

From my room in the ranch hotel I caught the strains of one very lovely song, a favorite of Mrs. Hohu's, translated by another great Hawaiian authority, Mary Kawena Pukui. The song tells of Hana, the coastal wind, and a kind of pungent seaweed known as *līpoa:*

> *White with the mist is the rain of Hana,*
> *Companion of the Malualua breeze.*
> *Two of us stood up on the summit;*
> *The third there was the fragrance of the līpoa.*

One can scarcely visit Hana without wondering how long its gentle small-town atmosphere can survive in the turmoil of fast-changing and developing Hawaii. Certainly it is worth trying to preserve. One morning I rode in a truck with Edmund Kalalau, a top paniolo on the ranch, as he transferred half a dozen Herefords from one lush seaside pasture to another. The route led us twice through town and Edmund rarely got both hands on the wheel, so many people waved to him as we passed. I mentioned my impression of a large family rather than a small town, and Edmund nodded shyly.

"It is one thing to drive through a place where you know everybody," he said. "It is another thing to like nearly all of them."

In one degree or another the same might be said of the entire coastal region of East Maui. Dominated by the giant mass of Haleakala volcano, the land becomes one great sloping shield of high mountain forest, gradually blending with the lighter shades of lowland fields swept now and

Engineer attaches a camera to a 60-inch reflecting telescope; a computer aims the giant eye. The Department of Defense sponsors this tracking station at "Science City" (below), near the summit of 10,023-foot Haleakala volcano. There students of the upper atmosphere and beyond take advantage of skies usually free of clouds, mist, dust or haze. Occupants include the Smithsonian Institution, the University of Hawaii, and the Atomic Energy Commission.

Signaling for silence, teen-age hunter Terry Lind listens for distant commotion that will tell him his dogs have cornered a wild pua'a—*pig. After the kill John English (in cap) and Joe Daniels wait as the dogs lap the blood. The hunts help conserve soil, for pigs root up and trample vegetation, hastening erosion.*

NATIONAL GEOGRAPHIC PHOTOGRAPHER JAMES L. AMOS (ABOVE)
AND DAVID R. BRIDGE, NATIONAL GEOGRAPHIC STAFF

then by gentle mist from the sea. In the folds and crevices of the shore-line small fishing villages nestle like fragments of bleached coral cast up and wedged among the dark shapes of boulders.

It is a beautiful and solitary land, one that draws its people together over long distances and across the years. Despite their isolation the villages have ties that run deep and often unseen. Josephine Medeiros gave me an example one day.

Josephine is the charming wife of Hana's chief of police. She was born and reared in the village of Keanae on East Maui's remote northern coast. As a girl Josephine was as gay and sociable as she is now, and she had many friends in the other villages. Now and then one of the friendships developed into a romantic attachment. Josephine recalls one boy with particular fondness.

"He lived several villages away," she told me, "but we managed to see a good bit of each other at community dances and at beach picnics here and there. People began taking us seriously and I guess the word got around, because my mother finally asked about him. We were in the kitchen one night and she said casually, 'What's this I hear about you and Harry So-and-so up in Kailua?' "

"Well, that started me off," Josephine said, smiling at the recollection. "I was about 17 at the time and I had some pretty romantic notions. I answered that we were deeply in love, that Harry was the most wonderful man in the whole world, it was the real thing and I couldn't live without him. Mother was very nice about it. She heard me out and then said quietly, 'Listen, dear, find somebody else; he's your second cousin.' "

Few outsiders with standard visions of progress can regard East Maui as anything but backward. Its miles of incomparable coastline and its great inland areas lie virtually unplanned and undeveloped, all but barren of major industry and construction. One of the reasons is Haleakala National Park, with its thousands of acres of protected reserve. Another reason is a 38-year-old former Marine helicopter pilot named Taylor A. Pryor, generally known as "Tap," whose Makai Corporation owns or controls 37,000 more acres in East Maui, including Hana Ranch and much of the town itself. By some people's standards Tap Pryor himself is a little backward.

So are his friends and fellow conservationists, men like Charles Lindbergh and Laurance Rockefeller, not to mention the people of Hana. All share a belief that Hawaii's natural assets are to be measured not in dollars and cents alone, but by what is left intact for future generations—a view regarded as obsolete by some developers.

"Actually, it's the standard approach to development that's obsolete," Tap told me in discussing Hana's future. "With the human explosion, we're past the time when we can allow technology to compete with environment—if there ever was such a time. The great loser in that competition can only be man. Instead, environment must become an integral part of technology, meaning not only that developers have to learn conservation but also that conservationists must become developers. It's the one moral as well as practical approach to the problem.

"Hawaii had that approach up until World War II," Tap continued. "Then it became a matter of duty and pride to expand as fast as we could, and we did it far too well. We were a provincial society, you see, and we didn't have the built-in restraints to handle growth on that scale. I believe we're finally getting those restraints, but it's a race with things like the new jumbo jets that threaten to make Hawaii just another suburb of Los Angeles."

I asked how he envisioned Hana in the future.

"Essentially as what it is now, a working community," he answered and then suddenly grinned. "Hawaiians *do* work, you know. Our leisurely vacationland image persists, and the idea of actually working in Hawaii is an international joke—I call it 'the Diamond Head syndrome.' But as far back as people here can remember, Hana has been a productive region. Not so long ago there were nine operating sugar mills in East Maui. Today the sugar industry is concentrated on the Other Side, but here we have ranching, a great commercial fishing potential, ideal conditions for agricultural and marine research institutions, and certainly all the ingredients for a major center of creative arts. And of course we have tourism, though not on such a massive scale that it dominates everything else. I don't think Hana would stand for that."

Against the day, however, when more outsiders discover the island, Hana is working hard to preserve the very best of its quiet beauty. With the help of Tap Pryor, his father Samuel Pryor, Lindbergh, Rockefeller, and other conservationists, a group in East Maui has carried out a successful effort to enlarge Haleakala National Park to include such natural

Varied bills of Hawaiian honeycreepers tell a story of evolution. Found only in the Hawaiian Islands, these 4- to 9-inch-long forest dwellers all belong to one family, the Drepanididae. Ornithologists believe they descended from a single species which came from America, and perhaps resembled the akepa (17). As competition for nectar and insects increased, more species of the birds evolved. Specialized beaks, developed through countless generations, helped them eat other foods. The hooked bill of the ou (12) scooped out ripe ieie fruit; Maui parrotbills (13) split twigs of the koa tree to search for grubs. Hard, dry seeds formed most of the diet of the Kona finch (16); its heavy beak readily cracked them open. The Kauai akialoa (9) probed its slender, curved bill deep into crevices of bark for tiny insects. Holding its mouth wide, the akiapolaau (8) hammered into rotten wood with its sturdy lower bill, then probed the openings for insects and larvae with its longer upper bill. Protected by the early

NED M. SEIDLER, NATIONAL GEOGRAPHIC STAFF

Hawaiians, who collected the feathers of the mamo (1) and the iiwi (3) to make capes for their kings, the honeycreepers declined in numbers after the influx of settlers following Cook's discovery. Mosquitoes, accidentally brought by ship, spread bird malaria; farmers cleared land and introduced predators, and the delicate balance of nature the honeycreepers depended on was upset. Within the last 80 years eight of the 22 species have become extinct, and today only the apapane (5) and the amakihi (11) remain common throughout the islands.

Common name, scientific name, and status of each of these species in Hawaii (all males): *1. Mamo,* Drepanis pacifica, *extinct. 2. Ula-ai-hawane,* Ciridops anna, *extinct. 3. Iiwi,* Vestiaria coccinea, *uncommon. 4. Crested honeycreeper,* Palmeria dolei, *extremely rare. 5. Apapane,* Himatione sanguinea, *common. 6. Anianiau,* Loxops parva, *rare. 7. Alauwahio,* Loxops maculata, *uncommon. 8. Akiapolaau,* Hemignathus wilsoni, *extremely rare. 9. Kauai akialoa,* Hemignathus procerus, *extremely rare. 10. Nukupuu,* Hemignathus lucidus, *extremely rare. 11. Amakihi,* Loxops virens, *common. 12. Ou,* Psittirostra psittacea, *extremely rare. 13. Maui parrotbill,* Pseudonestor xanthophrys, *extremely rare. 14. Laysan finch,* Psittirostra cantans, *common. 15. Palila,* Psittirostra bailleui, *rare. 16. Kona finch,* Psittirostra kona, *extinct. 17. Akepa,* Loxops coccinea, *rare.*

Taro patches spread over a seaside field near the village of Keanae. The plant arrived with the early islanders, and its cultivation became their major farming activity. Taro grows for about two years from planting to harvest; to assure an unfailing supply, Hawaiians till small plots planted throughout the year.

treasures as the Seven Sacred Pools, a stepping-stone series of volcanic basins on the island's south coast forever scoured and replenished by a mountain stream. I passed the area early one morning with Joe Daniels and two of his friends on our way to hunt *pua'a,* the Hawaiian pig.

Pua'a is both a blessing and a scourge to the islanders. On the one hand it provides endless main courses for luaus—the traditional Hawaiian feasts more accurately known as *pā'ina* or *aha'aina.* On the other, it ravages mountain vegetation to the point of causing serious erosion. While Hawaiians raise domestic pigs, they consider it a duty and a pleasure to track down the wild variety on foot in its mountain refuge. After one experience I'm inclined to think of it as mostly duty.

We left Hana at 4:30 a.m. in a pickup truck with the back full of boar hounds, and drove westward along the coast so as to reach the area known as Kaupo by sunrise. Mist draped the fields on either side with gauze, streaking the dark silhouettes of trees and softening the rough edges of the seaward cliffs. In the eerie half-light owls now and then ghosted from fence posts and drifted soundlessly away.

Behind us the sky turned from indigo to violet, with a thin seam of light where it joined the sea. Then the seam split along the horizon and night unraveled into the fiery brocade of a Pacific sunrise.

We parked the truck on Haleakala's lower slopes and started upward through heavily shadowed forest. Besides Joe and me there were Matthew Kalalau, the head groundskeeper at the hotel in Hana, and Terry Lind, a high-school junior and an expert hunter as well as owner of the hounds. It was Terry who carried the only gun, an ancient but well cared for single-shot .22-caliber rifle.

The moment we let the dogs down from the truck they vanished without a sound in the forests above us. As we hiked after them Joe explained that good boar hounds hunt in silence and that only when they have cornered pua'a does the commotion begin.

"Then you run," Joe said, "and you keep running till you get there, because you don't know whether it's a sow or a boar. If it's a sow there's not so much risk to the hounds, but a boar can lay one open with a single sweep of his tusks, and the rest will keep crowding in just the same. Look there, and you'll get an idea of what those tusks can do."

He pointed to the base of a tree where a wide patch of bark had been worn away, revealing a smooth under layer with great creases nearly an inch deep. "Pua'a scratches his hide against the bark," Joe said, "and when the bark comes loose he hones his tusks on the wood. Actually, the old boars are less dangerous to hounds than the young ones, because the tusks tend to curl back with age. It's the straight short tusks that are murder. The old boars, however, have fantastically tough hides. I've seen a .22 bullet bounce off a shoulder at fairly close range."

For half an hour more we trekked up the mountain in a stillness broken only now and then by the mournful trill of a Hawaiian dove. Often a heavy carpet of small guavas, called *waiawī,* made the footing as treacherous as a mud slide. I noticed patches of forest floor that had been churned and gouged as though by a giant disk harrow, indicating spots where pua'a had located choice beds of roots. It was beyond one of these that

Terry paused a moment to listen and then suddenly broke into a run.

The next four or five minutes are among the worst I can ever recall, for the hounds had cornered a pua'a half a mile away up a winding stream bed littered with loose stones and bordered by thick underbrush. With lungs bursting and legs on the point of collapse, I managed to reach the scene just as Terry got into position to fire.

The pig, a 150-pound sow, had backed into a culvert off the stream, holding the hounds at bay in the narrow defile. Abandoning the idea of a shot over the dogs' heads as too risky, Terry climbed onto a fallen tree directly above the sow and, reaching the rifle down as far as possible, put an end to the battle. Then he ordered the hounds away, and we all dropped to the ground to rest.

The sow proved similar to her domestic relatives except for a longer and coarser coat of brownish-gray hair. Lacking tusks, she had a set of very effective looking weapons in the sharp cloven hoofs on her forefeet. After Terry had driven the dogs away from the prize several times, they finally wandered off into the brush.

Ten minutes later, when we had caught our breath, I helped hold the carcass while Matthew Kalalau began to clean and dress it. It was then that we heard the dogs again, this time from a great distance.

My memory is mercifully vague on that second steeplechase, but it involved several high ridges overgrown with thick brush and paved with innumerable ripe guavas. The hounds had cornered a young 250-pound boar, and only Terry's speed and quick aim saved them from injury. It was a long time before any of us got his wind back.

When it came at last to packing the dressed-out carcasses down the mountainside I refused to be excused as a guest. My share of the job amounted to a stretch of about a mile with a hundred pounds of rather gamy sow slung over my back. I finally made it, half walking and half skidding on fallout from the guava trees. It was a week or two before I could look at pork again—or at guava jelly, for that matter.

The carcasses were set aside for a birthday party in honor of Joe's aunt the following week, but I was due next day in West Maui and missed the celebration. Joe has promised me a luau if I come back to Hana, and I intend to take him up on it. But somebody else has got to catch the pig.

The first day after leaving Hana I found myself back on Haleakala, but under somewhat less strenuous circumstances. Checking into a hotel at the town of Lahaina on Maui's western tip, I began a week's stay by driving east across the isthmus to the volcano's summit and paying a brief visit to "Science City."

Painted hearts mark the Lady of Fatima Shrine at Wailua. Worshipers say that in 1860 the sea washed up just enough coral and sand where none had existed to complete the church building. Older beliefs survive as well on Maui's northeast coast. Mrs. Mary Ann Pahukoa (above) is convinced that Hi'u, a guardian shark-god, lives offshore and protects her village, Keanae.

Actually the "city" is only a thin scattering of buildings perched on the crater rim, but there is no question about its scientific character. Its tenants include such organizations as the Atomic Energy Commission, the University of Hawaii, the Smithsonian Institution, and a civilian unit of the Department of Defense called the Advanced Research Projects Agency Maui Optical Station, happily abbreviated to AMOS.

In one way or another, all take advantage of Haleakala's 10,023-foot height and exceptionally clear atmosphere to study earth's upper regions and the endless sweep of space beyond. AMOS also studies the strange objects man puts there.

Just whose objects they are I never learned, for Glen Rogers wouldn't discuss it. Judging by what he was able to show me, they include both satellites and burned-out rockets, probably not all of them ours.

Glen is an optical engineer with Lockheed Missiles & Space Company, which operates AMOS under government contract with technical direction from another company, AVCO Everett Research Laboratory. He welcomed me to the station and explained that most of it was out of bounds but that he could show me one telescope I might find interesting.

It was quite an understatement, for Glen's telescope does things no ordinary mechanism could begin to match. As a rule, astronomical telescopes are geared to the earth's rotation, enabling them to lock onto a celestial target and to sweep mechanically from horizon to horizon in about 12 hours' time. AMOS's telescope does essentially the same thing, but its targets cross the sky in a matter of seconds. It can track a jet aircraft flying at high speed only a mile away. Such jobs call for tremendous power as well as precision, for the telescope and its synchronized dome together weigh a quarter of a million pounds.

For a demonstration Glen led me down a corridor and up two flights of stairs to the observation platform beneath a huge metal dome. In the center stood the telescope, an immense instrument with a 60-inch mirror, but seemingly no different from half a dozen I had seen.

"It's not much different," Glen said, "until it starts moving. It weighs about 15 tons, but it's beautifully balanced and suspended. Give it a swing yourself and you'll see."

Plump hinalea, one of more than 350 species of Hawaiian food fish, loses its colors as it dies.

I placed my hands against the base and shoved in a clockwise direction. Nothing happened at first, but as I gradually overcame inertia, the telescope began to swing smoothly around on its pedestal. "Try and stop it," Glen said. One might as well have tried to slow the earth's rotation, the momentum was so great. I quickly gave up.

"Now stand over here with me and let's see what the machinery can do," Glen suggested, moving to a large console against one wall. Adjusting half a dozen dials and tripping several switches, he pressed a final button and turned back to the telescope.

The world around us erupted into violent motion as a viewing panel in the dome overhead yawned open and the telescope began to sweep about like the arm of a huge crane moving at top speed. The noise of the dome was incredible, for with each swing of the telescope barrel the entire structure rotated on its giant bearings to keep the viewing window always in the direct line of aim. The effect of such mass and force together was overwhelming. When at last Glen switched off the power, I felt as if I had survived a terrible earthquake.

Later over coffee Glen told me a little more about the telescope. No human eye, of course, could remain trained to the viewpiece during an operation such as I had witnessed. As in much of astronomy today, highly sensitive instruments take over the job, storing the data in the form of permanent records for scientists to study. It is here that the AMOS telescope borders on science fiction, for it can virtually detect a fly in the sky.

At the base of the instrument, Glen explained, lies something called a sensor, an extremely delicate instrument for measuring infinitesimal amounts of light energy.

Since satellites and other orbiting objects are often visible to the unaided eye, I asked why AMOS needed such sensitive measurements.

"Have another cup of coffee," Glen said smiling.

As befits an island named after a demigod who stole fire from the gods, Maui is almost constantly in flames. The pyrotechnics have nothing to do with volcanoes but with another symbol of Hawaii, known to the ancient inhabitants as *kō* and to their English-speaking successors as sugarcane. Firing the cane fields is a preliminary step to harvesting, almost a year-round process in the 50th State.

Unlike other Hawaiian symbols such as the pineapple, the ukulele, and the guitar—all three of which are non-Polynesian imports less than 160 years old in the islands—kō arrived with the early settlers centuries ago. The first Hawaiians planted the giant species of grass as bordering hedges around their homes and lands. Now and then they broke off a stalk to chew for its sweet juice.

Poised to cast a throwing net, a fisherman peers intently into surf on Maui's east coast.

Astonishingly, it was to be more than a thousand years before the islanders began crushing cane in sizable amounts and boiling the juice down for crystallized sugar. The first real mill in Hawaii was established on Kauai in 1836; today Hawaii leads the islands in production, with Maui second and Kauai third.

A major reason for Maui's position is the Hawaiian Commercial & Sugar Company, better known as HC&S, whose headquarters are located at Puunene, in the valley that divides Maui's two great volcanic masses. With Kenneth Willey, the company's field director, I spent a morning inspecting the vast growing, harvesting, and processing operations of HC&S.

From Ken I learned that despite the relatively small area devoted to sugarcane—242,476 acres—the 50th State produced more than 3 percent of the world's raw cane sugar in 1968, or 1,232,182 tons. HC&S, the giant in the islands, accounts for nearly a sixth of Hawaii's total. Skill combined with climate has given Hawaiian growers the highest average annual yield in the world, as much as 11.12 tons of raw sugar per acre.

Our tour began with fields of seed cane, separately tended stalks that are grown for nine months, then cut into 18-inch lengths and planted to produce the actual harvest, known as crop cane. We traced the latter through fields of varying ages to maturity, where within two years the cane stands 12 to 15 feet high and is ready for harvesting. Afterward it may be allowed to grow again to produce a second or even a third harvest, each known as a "ratoon crop," after the ratoon, or sprout, remaining underground. With delightful humor Hawaiian parents often refer affectionately to children born to them late in life as their ratoon crop.

At every stage, sugarcane requires enormous quantities of water, far more than West Maui's annual 20 inches of rainfall can supply.

"It takes half a million gallons of water to produce a single ton of raw sugar," Ken said, "and we don't get anything like that. We draw it instead from the mountains and, to a small degree, from wells. With 29,505 acres under cultivation we use 180 billion gallons of water a year for irrigation —almost six times as much as Honolulu uses."

We watched several fields being burned off prior to harvest, each one protected from adjoining rows by gangs of workers patrolling the wide utility roads that double as firebreaks. Ken explained that far from damaging the stalks, flash-fire merely removes excess weight in the form of cane trash and leaves.

For those who envision the picturesque sugarcane harvester of old, wading through a field with his flashing machete, today's methods of gathering the crop are sadly lacking in romance. The bulldozer and the crane have replaced the man with the knife, and more than anything else a harvesting team resembles a road-construction crew. Ken and I watched as massive D-8 Caterpillar tractors chewed their way through acres of cane, sheering the stalks off at ground level with devices like huge dinner forks attached to their front ends. Other cranes delivered the harvest in great bundles to the cane haulers, diesel-powered and rubber-tired monsters the size of small ranch houses, each capable of carrying a 55-ton load to the mill.

The mill at Puunene is a giant version of a modernized kitchen, with grinders and blendors, rinsing tanks and pressure cookers, and one device reminiscent of the laundry—a great spin-drier designed to separate molasses from sugar crystals in the same way water is removed from a load of wash.

By far the most startling aspect of a modern mill is that in order to make sugar one generally adds sugar.

"It's a matter of crystallization," explained Edwin Ogasawara, the mill superintendent and a friend of Ken's. "Before it reaches the separation process our sugar is in liquid form, suspended in a syrup with molasses. To extract it we must force it to crystallize under heat, but at that stage the sugar is very uncooperative. Left to itself it will crystallize in many different sizes, not in the uniform grade we want. So we add a little powdered sugar to the syrup as a standard base around which the new sugar can crystallize evenly." Mr. Ogasawara beamed. "After that, everything cooperates beautifully."

If the Big Island is the Texas of Hawaii, Lahaina is its Nantucket or New Bedford, the Polynesian version of an old Yankee whaling town. In its day Lahaina rivaled even New Bedford in the number of whaling ships that called; the year 1846 brought 429 ships to the West Maui port. All were part of the great Yankee whale fishery that flourished in the 19th century, until the Civil War crippled it and petroleum eventually administered the death blow.

Lahaina prospered for many years as a base and a port of call whose

Directing with her right hand as she strikes a note with her left, Mrs. Mar-
tha Hohu conducts a rehearsal at the village of Hana. Each week she flies from
Honolulu to coach the amateur choir in traditional Hawaiian music. The com-
munity's aloha spirit, and its idyllic setting on the remote east coast of
Maui, inspired the nickname that titled a popular song: "Heavenly Hana."

virtue—or rather lack of it—was symbolized by James A. Michener in his novel *Hawaii* with a verse attributed to whalers:

> *I want to go back to Owhyhee,*
> *Where the sea sings a soulful song,*
> *Where the gals are kind and gentle*
> *And they don't know right from wrong!*

Unhappily for the whalers, another New England export arrived almost at the same time in Lahaina—a stern brand of Congregationalist faith brought by American missionaries from Boston. Reaching Hawaii in 1820, the missionaries settled in Honolulu, Kailua, Waimea, and Lahaina and proceeded to convert the islanders.

Under attack from Christianity, and with the help of the Hawaiian monarchy, the ancient system of kapus crumbled. Christian kapus promptly took their place, including several that dealt specifically with the habits of visiting whalers.

Outraged, the whalers responded with threats and curses. On one occasion they opened fire with a ship's cannon on the house of a missionary, proving themselves more at home with the harpoon than with powder and shot. The missionaries escaped injury and gradually won the town over. Lahaina became an outpost of Christianity in the islands.

Lahaina today is engaged in recapturing the picturesque elements of that vanished era, while drawing increasing numbers of tourists to its excellent hotels and restaurants, and its colorful shops. With Keith Tester

Cane-burner fires a sugar field (opposite) near the town of Puunene to burn off the leaves, making the ripened stalks easier to process. Cane haulers (below) carry the crop to the mill. Maui produces about a fourth of Hawaii's sugar.

Maui's wild, wild east: Veiled by wayside flowers, Herefords drift down a road on the 30,000-acre Ulupalakua Ranch. "The island's frontier," author Graves calls the eastern slopes of Haleakala volcano, "where cattle thrive in lush pastures overlooking the sea." At left, his kaula'ili, or lasso, on his saddle, a paniolo—cowboy—in a yellow slicker hazes stock out of a corral bordered by thick vegetation. Ranchers prod animals bound for Hawaii's markets through a cutting chute (opposite, upper) to grade them according to quality and age.

of the privately supported Lahaina Restoration Foundation I spent an afternoon exploring relics of the town's missionary era as well as of its seafaring past and of the monarchy. The foundation is preserving or reconstructing several historic buildings along original lines.

One landmark that needs no restoration is Lahainaluna High School, the famous missionary academy founded in 1831. Popular legend says it drew early pupils from such distant sources as the families of the California forty-niners, who preferred to send their children across 2,400 miles of open Pacific rather than have them risk the wilds of North America to reach eastern schools. Lahainaluna still flourishes on its hill overlooking the town—the oldest American school west of the Rockies, with a student body today of 600.

Despite their admirable work, the missionaries and their descendants have often been accused of profiteering from their connection with the Hawaiian monarchy, especially in the time of Kamehameha II and III. The charge recalls a somewhat similar complaint made by a poet and humorist against the first New Englanders: "The pilgrims...fell upon their knees, and then upon the aborigines."

"It's true that great fortunes in the islands were built up by the descendants of the early missionaries," Keith said. "But those first missionaries were dedicated people who stuck to their original purpose, one that involved great personal sacrifice. The monarchy rewarded the missions in the only way it knew how, with acreage. In many cases the second and third generations did break away and go into business or government, but only a few started with the original land grants. By and large they were honest, hard-working men, and they did as much in their way for Hawaii as their fathers before them."

· Opponents of the missionaries often overlook the brutal character of Hawaiian life in the pre-Christian era. One man who did not, and who summed it up with unforgettable humor and poignance, was that adoptive son of the islands, Mark Twain. In his book *Roughing It* Twain described pagan Hawaii as:

> ...a place where human sacrifices were offered up in those old bygone days when the simple child of nature, yielding momentarily to sin when sorely tempted, acknowledged his error when calm reflection had shown it him, and came forward with noble frankness and offered up his grandmother as an atoning sacrifice—in those old days when the luckless sinner could keep on cleansing his conscience and achieving periodical happiness as long as his relations held out; long, long before the missionaries braved a thousand privations to come and make them permanently miserable by telling them how beautiful and how blissful a place heaven is, and how nearly impossible it is to get there; and showed the poor native how dreary a place perdition is and what unnecessarily liberal facilities there are for going to it; showed him how, in his ignorance, he had gone and fooled away all his kinfolks to no purpose....

Despite his very real admiration for the missionaries, however, Twain could not resist a parting shot at them for having introduced the Hawaiians to the doctrine of sin and its consequences. During a visit to the Big Island he wrote, "How sad it is to think of the multitudes who have gone

"One of the breathing holes of hell," a minister wrote of Lahaina, where more than 400 whaling ships a year once anchored for refitting and recreation. Today's more sedate town preserves and rebuilds relics of its turbulent past. Above, the square-rigged bark Carthaginian rests at the pier before the Pioneer Inn; in the movie "Hawaii," her whalers defied missionary efforts to reform Lahaina. At left, a couple relaxes outside the hotel.

to their graves in this beautiful island and never knew there was a hell."

For some, the exact opposite of hell is West Maui's Kaanapali coast, often referred to by Hawaiians as the Gold Coast—several miles of glittering beach with an opulent array of condominium apartments, golf courses, and luxury hotels that attract more than half of Maui's annual visitors, estimated to reach 386,000 in 1970. Gold Coast developers proudly point out that when completed the 850-acre complex will contain 3,500 hotel rooms, while Waikiki Beach, with about the same area, has at least five times that number of rooms.

As long as Hawaii's tourist trade continues its geometric explosion, Kaanapali is one of the most attractive ways of handling it—a self-contained garden-style community for transients separated from other urban areas. With the spectacle of Honolulu's coastal sprawl in mind, Maui's planners have decreed that major development in the future will be limited to three areas of their island: the Lahaina-Kaanapali region; the county seat, Wailuku, with its neighboring city of Kahului; and the Kihei area along the south shore of the island's isthmus.

Of the three, Lahaina-Kaanapali attracts the broadest spectrum of visitors, from surfers and itinerant bands of hippies to wealthy mainland families bent on days of golfing, sunbathing, and leisurely swimming.

Occasionally the swimming leads to unexpected adventures. Some months ago a teen-age girl from the mainland was enjoying an afternoon sunbath aboard an oversize raft just offshore near Kaanapali. The day was tranquil and the sunlight warm. Presently a young man she knew swam out from the beach and joined her. The two talked for a while and then fell asleep to the gentle rocking of the raft. They were awakened when the rocking became more than gentle.

While they slept, the raft had drifted far offshore, into the waters of Auau Channel, the nine-mile-wide strait separating Maui from the Island of Lanai. Once out of the lee of Maui the raft had picked up speed under the relentless thrust of the northeast trades and was now rollicking along toward the distant outline of Lanai. There was no hope of paddling back to shore. Then the sun set and the wind rose to gale force.

Old-timers in the islands still marvel that the couple survived, and in fact they spent more time off the raft than on it. In the darkness and seething rush of angry waves they capsized repeatedly, almost losing their grip on the raft. Often the hold of one barely saved the other. At some point during the night—the girl could not recall when—the nightmare force of the water stripped away her bathing suit.

Without Lanai the pair would unquestionably have been lost. Driven before the wind on a direct course to the island, they washed ashore before dawn on that graveyard of many a vessel, Lanai's Shipwreck Beach. Half dead, they collapsed on the sand, where the islanders eventually found them. No stretch of coast, the two said later, ever looked more beautiful. But then perhaps they had never seen Molokai.

Surfcasting at sunset, a fisherman ducks into the spray of a wave crashing onto Maui. Proud of their island's solitary beaches and booming resorts, forest-clad mountains and fertile farms, residents boast, "Maui no ka oi"—Maui is best.
GORDON W. GAHAN

MOLOKAI, LANAI, KAHOOLAWE

A child of the gods, pineapples by the million, and an island gunnery range

IN A STATE where nicknames are an inevitable part of geography, one might call them the "Forgotten Islands" or the "Neglected Islands." Few tourists are familiar with the charms of Molokai and its people, and fewer still with those of Lanai. As for Kahoolawe, hardly a score of visitors set foot there in a year's time, for it is under constant fire as a target range by the U. S. Navy and Marine Corps.

Historically, Molokai holds little claim to its present title, the "Friendly Island." In ancient times its priests were among the most dreaded in all Hawaii for their power and their devotion to the sacrificial altar. Later Molokai developed an even more dreadful image as a place of exile for the living dead—those afflicted with *ma'i-Pākē*, the Hawaiian term for "Chinese disease," known to Westerners as leprosy.

All three islands are legally part of the county of Maui, though they contribute less than a quarter of its population: some 6,000 on Molokai and roughly half that on Lanai. Kahoolawe's only permanent residents are wild goats that roam the island's scarred and tortured hills in random herds, nimbly foraging between air strikes and naval target practice.

Honorary mayor of Molokai, Mitchell Pauole greets visitors at the island's airport. His button announces Molokai's nickname; his warm smile confirms it. He wears a lei of rickrack and pearl beads and a shirt unmistakably Hawaiian.

Kalaupapa, dwindling village of exile, lies on the north shore of Molokai. Since 1866 Hawaiians afflicted with Hansen's disease — leprosy — have gone into isolation on the remote peninsula. Today drugs control the condition, and no new patients come to the colony. At right, author Graves talks with Cecilia and James Davidson, whose cases have been arrested.

In size the trio stands near the bottom of Hawaii's scale. Among the state's eight major islands Molokai ranks fifth with 261.1 square miles, Lanai is sixth with 139.5, and Kahoolawe last with 45. Lonely Niihau, off the Island of Kauai, ranks seventh with 73 square miles.

Molokai, however, has something better than mere size—she is a true child of the gods, the only daughter of Wakea, father of islands, and the beautiful goddess Hina. Happily for Molokai, she inherited her mother's beauty and a good deal of her father's divine influence: *Moloka'i pule o'o*, runs an old Hawaiian adage, meaning roughly, "The prayers of Molokai are answered."

Now and then Molokai provides the answers to her own prayers, as I learned before setting foot on the island. Through the courtesy of the Royal Hawaiian Air Service, an inter-island line that combines travel with a touch of sightseeing, I had a low-level tour of Molokai on the flight between Maui's Kaanapali coast and Molokai's small central airport northwest of the town of Kaunakakai. The pilot offered me the seat next to him on the half-hour trip by twin-engine Cessna.

Crossing Pailolo Channel, we approached Molokai on its majestic windward side. Here the island bursts abruptly from the sea in a colossal rampart of 2,000-foot-high cliffs notched by half a dozen great valleys and overgrown with jungle, resembling the ruined walls of some sacked and abandoned fortress. Driving in from the northeast, the trade winds tirelessly continue the assault, drenching the coast with torrential showers and streaking the massive headland with the bright veins of innumerable waterfalls. One of these, Kahiwa Falls, plunges 1,750 feet in several spectacular stages to the sea, giving Hawaii its highest cascade.

Back of the cliffs the land slopes gently upward in a series of plateaus to a single great ridge running nearly half the length of the island and gradually tapering off into dry plains at the western end.

In its very beauty lies one of Molokai's major problems: how to bring water and people together. The island's population, along with its ranching and agricultural industries, is concentrated in the lowland areas of the south and west, rarely touched by rain. On Molokai's uninhabited windward coast spectacular streams and falls drain precious water into the sea at the rate of some 150,000,000 gallons a day, siphoning off Molokai's major hope of development.

"Take a good look at those falls while you can," the pilot told me. "Molokai has a new project designed to dry some of them up and divert the water to the other side of the island. In just a minute you'll see what they plan to collect it in."

Skimming westward, we crossed the flat spur of land on Molokai's northern coast with its village of Kalaupapa, the isolated colony for 168 victims of leprosy, now generally referred to as Hansen's disease. Once again I noted along one edge of the peninsula the small airstrip that I had seen weeks before from an Air Force jet.

"You can reach the village by climbing down a narrow trail from the top of the cliffs, where some of the medical staff live," the pilot said, "but it's much simpler to catch a morning flight to Kalaupapa from Molokai's airport. The people at the colony will be glad to show you around."

Contingent of Peace Corps volunteers on Molokai's southeast coast trains for assignment in Western Samoa. In an outdoor classroom (above), an instructor from the University of Hawaii Peace Corps Training Center schools students in sanitation. Below left, corpsmen learn how to install a simple toilet. A Samoan-language teacher (below right) helps prepare the recruits for duty in her country. Technical training, cultural studies, and public-health education keep trainees busy during 12-hour days. Seminars and group discussions often last into the night. In 12 weeks the corpsmen will embark on a new way of life. Opposite, soft ocean breezes dry laundry outside the dormitory.

Beyond Kalaupapa the cliffs subsided and we turned inland above rolling hills cross-stitched with irrigated pineapple fields and giving way now and then to stretches of virtual desert. Over one of the latter we came on a huge depression in the earth, shaped like a squared-off frying pan and glistening with the same metallic sheen in the morning sun.

"That's the new reservoir for the diversion project," the pilot said. "The lining is a thin sheet of nylon-reinforced butyl rubber laid down to prevent seepage—Molokai's soil is volcanic and it leaks like a sieve. Incidentally, that's the largest rubber-lined reservoir in the whole world. If you're interested in it, look up George Harada in Kaunakakai. He's the irrigation-system manager for Molokai and he can tell you all about it."

George did better than that. The next afternoon he took me into the reservoir to see the last of the lining being put in place and to explain what the diversion system—known as the Molokai Irrigation Water Project—means to the future of the island.

"In plain figures," George said, "it means nearly a billion and a half gallons of water on tap in a place that has suffered from thirst since time began." He gestured toward the distant ridge running east of us.

"Underneath that ridge we've built a huge underground aqueduct capable of delivering 25,000,000 gallons of water a day from the wet side of the island over here to the dry side. It just happens that winter is the season of heaviest rain on the wet side, but summer is the time we need water most—for agriculture, ranching, and for a future tourist industry. Once the reservoir and the aqueduct are linked together, we'll have a huge constant supply instead of a torrent one month and a trickle the next. In the long run it could mean a new life for Molokai, with higher income, new industry, and more people to enjoy one of the loveliest and least-known islands in Hawaii."

We inspected one edge of the lining, a vast sheet of pliant, slightly silvery material that already covered two-thirds of the reservoir. Some of the 75 workers on the lining project were laying the rubber down in slightly overlapping sheets, each 600 feet long, more than 13 feet wide, and 1/32 of an inch thick. Other workers followed behind, applying rubber adhesive and strips of gummed material to the seams, weighting the sheet down against the wind with sandbags until the day when tons of water would hold it in place.

George introduced me to Vernon Funn, project engineer for the Department of Land and Natural Resources, who reeled off additional figures on the reservoir: capacity, roughly 1,400,000,000 gallons; area of the excavation, 104 acres; total amount of rubber for the lining, 810 tons. Not only is it the world's biggest rubber-lined reservoir, but it also is the largest of any kind in Hawaii.

It gradually dawned on me that the great majority of the overalled workers were women. I asked Mr. Funn if men were in short supply.

Pineapple fields surround the new Kualapuu Reservoir, built to irrigate 16,000 arid acres on Molokai. An underground aqueduct brings water from the windward coast. During construction, 67,000 sandbags anchored the butyl-rubber lining (right) as workers prepared seams for sealing with adhesives.

"Not at all," he answered, smiling. "Men do the heavy work of delivering the rolls of rubber where they're needed, but then the women take over. The joining operation is basically a sewing job and women still run the straightest seam, whether they're lining a dress or a reservoir."

While Molokai looks forward to new ways of life, other, tragic, ways are passing. Since the dawn of history the mysterious scourge of leprosy has condemned its victims to purgatory on earth, a shadow life of loneliness and suffering in exile from other men behind the barriers of ignorance and fear. Among Hawaiians the names Kalaupapa and Kalawao commemorate one of the darkest chapters in island history. But they also commemorate the shining spirit of a man called Joseph.

He was Joseph de Veuster, but the world knows him as Father Damien, an unassuming Belgian priest who made his way to the islands in 1864. After a visit to Kalaupapa in 1873, he began the work that 16 years later would claim his life. By pagan and Christian alike in Hawaii he is revered as a saint, for almost singlehandedly he ministered to the physical and spiritual needs of those whom other men had abandoned.

Gingerly avoiding toxic spines, divers bag a crown-of-thorns starfish (Acanthaster planci). *Feeding on coral polyps, the predator threatens reefs across the Pacific.*

In Damien's time the trip to Kalaupapa — or rather to its forerunner, the nearby village of Kalawao — was arranged via ship by the Hawaiian monarchy with neither the traveler's consent nor his return passage.

Like most other present-day visitors, I reached Kalaupapa by the 10-minute supply flight from Molokai's airport. I had received permission for the trip from Hawaii's Department of Health, which manages the colony. From the air Kalaupapa appears no different from a hundred other coastal villages in the islands, with its brief network of paved streets and its clusters of houses shaded by soft canopies of trees and bordered by rows of flower beds. Even from within the village, life at first seems normal. Then subtle differences gradually register on the outsider, not in terms of what he sees but rather what he finds missing. For Kalaupapa lacks certain things that other villages consider essential. I discovered several of them, along with the reasons, during a visit with Cecilia Davidson.

Cecilia is a patient at Kalaupapa who works as a guide for the colony. She has suffered from Hansen's disease through many years and she keeps it no secret from visitors. Few would guess the fact simply from her minor scars. She had agreed by phone the day before to show me around the village where she has lived since 1941.

I found her waiting beside the airstrip — a woman of late middle age and gentle good looks, obviously with some Polynesian and perhaps Oriental blood. It was only later that I noticed the slight erosion of one eyelid and faint areas of paler skin around her left elbow. By that time, however, I knew her better and I had changed my mind about her looks: To me Cecilia is very nearly beautiful.

Before visiting Kalaupapa, I had done some reading on the disease Cecilia suffers from and was surprised by what I learned. For one thing,

Hansen's disease—named after the Norwegian discoverer of the bacillus that causes it—rarely kills of itself, though it weakens the body's resistance to other infections. Of two types, one affects the nerves, leading to atrophy and frequent amputation of the extremities; the other produces ulcers and thickening of the skin.

For a mildly infectious disease it is mysteriously inconsistent. It is never directly inherited, and is transmitted between husband and wife in fewer than 10 percent of cases. Yet in the past a child born of leprous parents who remained in close contact with them or with other patients had a 40 percent chance of contracting the disease. Today a child who is removed from contact at birth runs virtually no risk at all.

No one knows with certainty how Hansen's disease is transmitted, nor has anyone managed it artificially: Laboratory experiments with inoculation have invariably failed. Close contact in itself is no answer—among hundreds of doctors, nurses, and attendants connected with Kalawao and Kalaupapa over the years, only one ever developed Hansen's disease. The victim was Father Damien himself, and many Hawaiians believe he worked so hard for the colony that his resistance simply failed.

For thousands of years man was powerless to combat the disease, and even today there is no real cure. But in 1946 scientists began to use drugs of the family known as sulfones, which arrest it in most cases and reduce the dangers of transmission. The discovery brought hope into the darkest corner of Hawaiian life and foretold the end of Kalaupapa.

Voracious starfish—once a rarity, now a plague—intrigue divers. The explosive increase in their numbers remains unexplained.

"No new cases are sent to the colony," Cecilia explained after we had settled ourselves in her station wagon. "About 20 people a year develop Hansen's disease in Hawaii now, and they're all treated at a hospital near Honolulu—in isolation while the disease is active and as outpatients once it's been arrested." She smiled. "That's why I'm allowed to show you around and take you home to meet my husband. We've both been arrested cases for a long time and can't infect other people."

Out of Kalaupapa's 168 patients at the time of my visit 131 besides Cecilia and her husband were arrested cases, continuing with medication but leading more or less normal lives, depending on the degree of disability. I was to discover it took a considerable handicap to keep a villager idle. The remaining 35 patients either had failed to respond fully to drugs or had suffered recurrences and were isolated as infectious.

As we drove along Kalaupapa's quiet, narrow streets, I began to feel a curious and unaccustomed sense of order among the houses on either side and suddenly realized what was missing. No swings dangled from tree limbs, no bicycles leaned against gateposts, no wagons cluttered front walks, awaiting eager drivers. Kalaupapa plainly had no children.

"We haven't for many, many years," *(Continued on page 166)*

Overleaf: Low-lying clouds and morning mist break against the fluted mountains of Molokai's windward coast, where 2,000-foot cliffs plunge into the sea. Jungle scrub, vines, ferns, and thickets choke the rain-drenched uplands.

With 42 miles of arm-wrenching paddling ahead, contestants in the annual Molokai-Oahu Outrigger Canoe Race break from the starting area near Laau Point. Once out of the harbor and into the turbulent Kaiwi Channel, they may face 20-foot waves and gale winds. At intervals, relief men on escort boats will change places with the paddlers. Before the start (left), team members pledge their best effort. At the finish 6.5 hours later, spectators wade right in. A victor clasps his young son in triumph.

Cecilia remarked sadly. "Even in the old days we knew that youngsters ran a far higher risk of infection than adults, and many were taken away to become *hānai* — foster children — in the homes of relatives or friends on the outside. In 1930 it became the law: A child born at Kalaupapa must leave the same day and must not come back to visit at least till the age of 17. It's a good law — since 1930 not one such child has developed the disease.

"Of course," she added, "the rule matters less now, since no new patients come to Kalaupapa. The youngest person here is in her late 20's and the last child was born nine years ago. Probably there won't be another. It's sad, but terrible things happened in the days when we knew less about Hansen's disease. My husband remembers very well."

We toured the colony then, visiting an excellent small library, a well-equipped clinic, the craft shop, and the post offices. Kalaupapa's mail is handled in two separate buildings — one for the 50 staff members and the other for patients, whose outgoing shipments were once fumigated, a practice that has been discontinued.

Many of the colony's non-medical jobs are filled by patients themselves, whose genuine warmth and dignity distract the visitor's attention from mutilated eyelids, ears, and nostrils. Among other patients, however, a high degree of skill emphasizes deformity. In the craft shop I noticed one woman operating a heavy loom at high speed. Most of the fingers were missing from her hands.

Since arrested cases are permitted to leave Kalaupapa, I asked Cecilia why those with only minor disfigurement stayed on.

"It's not that easy for us on the outside yet," she answered. "People are still afraid of Hansen's disease, even when there's no danger, and it's difficult to get jobs. The state provides for us here and pays us each a regular allowance."

She swept a hand toward the rows of neat houses with their landscaping and flower beds, and at the soft blue of the sea beyond. "Besides, for many it is the only home they can remember."

Finally we stopped at Cecilia's house and I met her husband, a powerfully built man in his 50's with an extraordinarily gentle air and a quick, irresistible smile. Despite two badly deformed hands, each with several fingers missing, he was hurrying off to help a neighbor move a refrigerator and asked if I couldn't stay until evening. Unhappily I couldn't and he urged me to come back another time when the three of us could spend a day together. On the way to the airport Cecilia told me a little about him.

Born in the colony to parents who both suffered from Hansen's disease, he had been quickly removed, and allowed to return only a few times for brief visits as a child. In those days meetings were arranged in a large room at Kalaupapa with a large glass panel separating patients from visitors.

In the case of Cecilia's husband protective measures failed; he contracted the disease as a young man and entered Kalaupapa voluntarily in 1944. By that time both his parents were dead — in all his life he never touched or kissed them and scarcely knew the sound of their voices.

A far different type of scourge menaces Molokai's undersea regions. One morning I joined a group of divers on the island's south coast in

White rumps of pronghorns flash alarm as a band dashes across eroded bluffs on Lanai. Imported from Montana, the animals become fair game when they browse on tender pineapple shoots. On headlands and in brush coverts, island hunters also find wild turkey, pheasant, partridge, goats, sheep, and deer.

search of a possible threat to Hawaii's vital offshore coral reefs: *Acanthaster planci,* the voracious crown-of-thorns starfish. With Mike Givens, an expert scuba diver and the manager of the Hotel Molokai, I accompanied a team of marine biologists from the State Division of Fish and Game. They were investigating reports of a huge concentration of the coral-devouring multipedes, said to have appeared in Kalohi Channel between Molokai and the Island of Lanai.

We never found the colony—crown-of-thorns starfish can move several hundred feet a day, wiping out great stretches of reef as they go by digesting millions of tiny coral-building polyps. As yet Hawaii has suffered none of the devastation visited on such regions as Guam and Australia's Great Barrier Reef, but the 50th State stands to lose much of its undersea splendor as well as tourist revenue if the starfish reaches epidemic proportions there. I had seen scattered specimens of *Acanthaster* during the dive with Jim Robinson to the lava formations off the Big Island, but not in concentrations large enough to do serious harm.

After we had given up the search for *Acanthaster,* Mike showed me several of his favorite reefs at 60 and 70 feet in Kalohi Channel's crystal depths. The area is famous among sport fishermen and divers for its great variety of marine life. We shared the great ridges and canyons with schools of small *aku,* the graceful skipjack, with lumbering *ulua,* or pompano, with albacore and snapper. From time to time a torrent of mullet streamed by in massive flight from some larger enemy.

As always, there were the bright pennants of small reef fish fluttering from the crests and pinnacles of dark coral, as though in cheerful welcome to passersby. I couldn't help thinking that even under the sea, Molokai lives up to the nickname "Friendly Island."

In all Hawaii no island lives up more spectacularly to its second name than does Lanai. With the tireless rhythm of a production line the "Pineapple Island," as Hawaiians call it, plants, irrigates, harvests, and ships some 122,000,000 units of whole fruit a year to one of the great canneries at Honolulu. In turn Honolulu supplies more than half the world's pineapple, plus such side-products as cattle feed, and an enzyme, bromelain, used in pharmaceuticals and in food processing.

To maintain its share of the flow—roughly one-fifth of Hawaii's total—Lanai keeps a quarter of a billion pineapple plants under cultivation and men like Warner Hobdy in a state of perpetual motion.

At the time of my visit Warner was superintendent of harvesting on Lanai for the Dole Company, a division of Castle & Cooke that owns the island and employs virtually all of its 2,000 workers. He took a morning off from a busy schedule of conferences and reports to meet my flight from Molokai and give me an automobile tour of the world's largest pineapple plantation.

A complete view would take weeks, for Dole has nearly 24 square miles of pineapple fields on Lanai in various stages of growth covering a 22-month period. Autumn harvest had ended and Warner began our tour among the recently picked fields. Here teams of workers were gathering up "crowns"—clusters of spiny leaves attached to the tip ends of fruit—that had been broken off and left behind during harvest. The crowns are planted in freshly prepared fields to start a new crop; experienced field hands can set out as many as 1,000 an hour.

Recalling the highly mechanized sugarcane harvest on Maui, I asked Warner if similar techniques could be applied to pineapple.

"We wish they could," he answered. "In the long run it would save us a great deal of money. But harvesting pineapple is still a job for the human eye and hand. The fruit doesn't ripen uniformly, so we have to pick each field several times to get everything at just the right moment.

"We're working hard to develop a strain without any variations," he added, and then smiled. "Or as a woman visitor to Lanai put it recently: 'Dole is dedicated to the proposition that all pineapples can be created equal.' She's right, but I'm afraid it's still only a proposition."

Where water is in short supply, pineapple has a major advantage over sugarcane: It requires far less irrigation. To tap Lanai's limited reserves of water, engineers have drilled wells as deep as 1,270 feet on the island's heights and laid pipelines down to the leeward side. Here the Dole Company distributes water over the moss-green embroidery of fields with the world's most colossal self-propelled sprinkler. Topping a gentle rise, Warner braked the car to a stop and pointed to a machine at work in the fields below. Even from a distance the sight was spectacular.

The impression was one of some monstrous locust poised on a strip of grass, its transparent wings outstretched and fluttering as though for take-off. Warner drove down the slope and alongside the machine so I could get a close look at the wings. They turned out to be long sections of waterpipe, extending on either side of a heavy truck and fitted at intervals with powerful sprinklers trained toward the ground. The shimmer of spray in sunlight had produced the fluttering effect.

"It's designed to run between two pineapple fields," Warner explained, "irrigating on each side. No tank truck could hold enough water for the job, so drivers trail a long extension hose mounted on a reel in the machine and hook up to a succession of irrigation hydrants spaced around the fields. From tip to tip the waterpipes stretch 278 feet, which means you could run that machine across a football field at the 50-yard line and almost water the end zones!"

We finished the tour in Warner's office over a cup of coffee. I was hoping to sample a slice or two of Dole's famous product, but time passed and none appeared. At length I put aside manners and asked about it. He was very apologetic.

"I wish you'd come two weeks ago," he said, "I would have sent you off with a couple of bushels of the finest fruit you ever tasted in your life. But the harvest is over and everything's gone to Honolulu. To tell you the truth, there isn't a ripe pineapple anywhere on the island."

The last of the "forgotten" trio is Kahoolawe, the target range southeast of Lanai. I flew to it one day by helicopter with a detachment of Navy and Marine personnel from the air station at Kaneohe Bay on Oahu's east

Overleaf: Pineapple rules 15,000 acres of red earth at Dole Company's Lanai Plantation; 67-foot harvesting booms collect the fruit. Machines developed to speed work in the fields help make "pines" Hawaii's leading crop after sugar.

coast. I had been invited to watch a day's gunnery practice by two Canadian destroyers firing from four miles offshore at a make-believe convoy of abandoned trucks that constitutes one of the island's main targets.

Many others had preceded the Canadians, paving Kahoolawe's thinly forested slopes with the hardware of battle — tons of shell fragments, casings of air-to-ground missiles, burned-out parachute flares, 20-mm cannon cartridges, and the remains of a dozen other types of weapons. All were churned in with Kahoolawe's volcanic debris of scorched and tempered rocks, making it hard to distinguish between the violent handiwork of nature and man. In some cases the latter has proved ineffective, and Kahoolawe is littered with duds. Bill Harvey, a young Navy lieutenant in charge of our fire-control party, warned me not to stray from the clearly marked paths around the observation post.

The Canadians proved a bit rusty at first, firing as much as half a mile on either side of the target. Bill radioed corrections over a field transmitter, and gradually the bursts moved directly in among the trucks of the convoy. For a final exercise Bill radioed the destroyers to fire at a target involving what he called "danger element." I asked what that meant, and he answered, "It represents a target located next to friendly troops."

And where did one find friendly troops on a deserted island? "Right here," Bill said, indicating our observation post. "The destroyers are going to fire at that marker on the next hill. Let's hope they've got their eye now."

So we hoped, and they had, for the marker disappeared in a cloud of smoke, and I feel a very special fondness for Canadians.

I saw Molokai once more, during the great annual event known as the Molokai-Oahu Outrigger Canoe Race. The contest draws outrigger canoe teams from most of the major islands in a grueling 42-mile race across open sea between Molokai's western tip and the finish line near Honolulu's Waikiki Beach.

My hopes rode with the team from Kauai on the morning we all gathered — some by air and others by chartered or private boat — for the start near Molokai's Laau Point. I had met the Kauai team coach the night before, a soft-spoken and immensely likable man in his 40's named Stanford Achi.

Stan felt that Kauai had a good chance against the heavily favored teams of Oahu, such as Waikiki Surf, Outrigger Canoe Club, and Healani. As it turned out the favorites swept the field, but Kauai came in fourth, putting up a great battle, in the spirit of a moving invocation by the Reverend Abraham Akaka of Oahu just before the start:

"We thank Thee for the forces of our history that focus on this moment, for our forefathers in these islands whose legacy of love for the sea and skill in canoe-making and seamanship we have inherited . . .

"God go with you, every one."

Wading through pineapple plants, pickers snap off fruit and load it onto a belt that moves it to the collecting bin on the harvesting machine. To protect against the plants' spikes, workers wear long sleeves, caps, gloves, and goggles (above).

KAUAI

Waimea

Lihue

NIIHAU

KAUAI, NIIHAU,
THE LEEWARD CHAIN

Lonely splendor of the westward frontier

IT IS AS UNLIKELY A NAME as you will find for a warm and endlessly hospitable town—Lihue, meaning "cold chill." Nor does it apply any more readily to the surrounding island, for Kauai is one vast and sunlit garden whose ancient name many translate as "fruitful season." One look is enough to explain why.

It is a serious mistake to visit Kauai alone—and I didn't. My wife Louise joined me from Washington, D. C., for a 10-day stay on the island. There were times during the visit, however, when I thought I might have to *leave* alone, for Louise fell in love with Jack Harter—or rather, with Jack and his Fairchild-Hiller 1100. Jack is president and chief pilot of Garden Island Helicopters, a firm that specializes in delivering people and cargo to some of the most impossible and beautiful spots in the world, not to mention the State of Hawaii.

Kauai is the acknowledged *grande dame* among the major islands—a lady of great beauty in the fullness of her years. With more logic than chivalry, geologists estimate her span to be as great as 5,600,000 years— almost half again as old as her nearest rival, Oahu, and at least ten times

Watery chute in Kilauea Stream catapults a bather into a pool on Kauai. Streams flowing from 5,148-foot-high Mount Waialeale wrap the island in a green cloak trimmed with waterfalls. Lying to leeward, Niihau (map) gets little rain.

that of the Big Island. Everyone agrees that Kauai carries her age remarkably well. Her vital statistics are undistinguished: fourth-largest of the islands, containing 553.3 square miles, with an ample waistline of 110 miles at low tide; smallest population among Hawaii's four counties, with 31,200 inhabitants, plus another 250 on the neighboring Island of Niihau; and eighth-highest peak in the state, dormant Kawaikini, standing 5,243 feet above the sea.

One might as well give the exact dimensions of the Garden of Eden.

Inevitably, Hawaiians call it the "Garden Island," without specifying which garden they mean. Kauai is actually many in one, including seaside park, tropical arboretum, high-altitude marsh, and haunting desert landscape, all interspersed with an endless profusion of flowers.

Nor are Kauai's exotic specimens confined to plant life. The island is a vast sanctuary for Hawaii's dwindling native birds, harboring 10 of the state's 27 endangered species. The reason, apart from Kauai's wilderness areas, is the islanders' refusal to import the Indian mongoose as other Hawaiians did during the 19th century to control rats. The mongoose preferred more colorful fare, helping obliterate two dozen species of birds in a century and a half. As it happened, the remaining species provided Louise and me with an unforgettable introduction to Kauai.

Arriving by inter-island jet in Lihue, Kauai's county seat, we checked into the Kauai Surf Resort and called on Jack Harter at his office there. Ordinarily Jack conducts a fascinating one-hour helicopter tour of the island, with a brief stopover along the Na Pali Coast or in Waimea Canyon, the spectacular gorge chiseled by erosion out of Kauai's desertlike leeward slope. That day, however, Jack had other plans.

"I'm running a bird count with the U. S. Fish and Wildlife Service this afternoon," he said, "and you're both welcome to join us. It's a longer flight than usual and I think you'll like it. We'll be taking a look at Niihau, our off-limits island to the west, so you'll see something a little special. Then we'll swing around the western end of Kauai on the way home."

That afternoon at the heliport Jack introduced us to our fellow passenger, John Sincock, a Fish and Wildlife Service research biologist for Hawaii. We climbed into the Fairchild-Hiller and Jack lifted us smoothly off in a great sweeping arc over the roofs of Lihue.

Jack believes in sightseeing at point-blank range and he has the skill and judgment to manage it safely. Flying a hundred feet or so above the trees, he threaded a notch in Kauai's southeastern rampart of mountains and swung along the island's leeward coast. The land swept slowly beneath us as though under a powerful lens, and we had time to single out a number of details.

Against the coarse green weave of sugarcane fields an occasional village slipped by, its bright pattern of gardens and flowering trees looking like a centerpiece arranged on an immense tablecloth. At Poipu Beach along the island's southern rim we passed a slender colonnade of new resort hotels, built to absorb a large percentage of Kauai's 300,000 annual tourists. Half a dozen surfers were riding the modest offshore swells. As we whirled overhead, one of them waved a cheerful greeting and instantly paid for his gallantry with a spectacular wipe-out.

"Feeling peaceful with flowers" inspired Ray and Bettie Lauchis to give the name Olu Pua to the botanical gardens they created on Kauai. The two, busy in their "baby factory" — a shaded area for seedlings (below) — have introduced thousands of plants, collected rare local varieties, and turned their hillside into a fragrant retreat for visitors. Hibiscus (left) adorns many an ear because it lasts the day without water.

Hawaii's flowers, lovers of the tropics, traveled from many parts of the earth to find welcome at Olu Pua Gardens, Kauai. The stars of the red passion-vine (*Passiflora vitifolia*), opposite, shone in South America, and the red jade vine (*Mucuna bennettii*), with upcurved keels, upper right, made its home in the Philippines and New Guinea. From Brazil came a member of the periwinkle family, the yellow *Allamanda* (upper left). On the catwalk in her gossamer rigging, the shadow spider *(Argiope appensa)* waits for a meal to wing by. To the right of her, the bright panicles of *Cassia multijuga,* from South America, almost hide the tree's feathery green. At lower right, blooms of a *Billbergia* thrust from its sheath. It bears little resemblance to its American relative, Spanish moss. Official flower of the 50th State, the hibiscus (lower left) has been crossbred freely among exotic and native forms to produce more than 5,000 hybrids.

DAVID R. BRIDGE, NATIONAL GEOGRAPHIC STAFF (TWO PHOTOS LOWER LEFT) AND NATIONAL GEOGRAPHIC PHOTOGRAPHER JAMES L. AMOS

Over the small coastal town of Waimea, Jack banked inland, skirting the shallow bay where Captain Cook first set foot in the islands. Then we were between the great jaws of Waimea Canyon, lifting sharply with the land toward the western shoulder of Waialeale volcano and its giant catch basin, the remote Alakai Swamp.

It is here that the trade winds, as though in a parting gesture to Hawaii, loose a cascade of water averaging more than 40 feet a year, baptizing Waialeale as the rainiest spot on earth and scouring Waimea Canyon ever deeper with the runoff. Unlucky Niihau, directly in the lee of Kauai, gets a mere sprinkling of leftovers and is forced to barge additional water from its neighbor island across 10 miles of intervening channel.

"John and I are going to check the rain gauge on Waialeale and take a quick look around for birds," Jack said to Louise and me over the intercom. "Why don't you two have a balcony seat in the canyon and we'll pick you up in 15 minutes."

It was a balcony beyond the dreams of a steeplejack, the weathered crown of a solitary butte thrusting nearly half a mile above the center of the canyon floor and tapering at the peak to a level area no bigger than a tennis court. Luckily for Louise, she scarcely had time to see it, for Jack approached the butte from below, easing gently over the crest and touching down quickly with hardly a bump.

Louise and I climbed out and stood on a broad ledge below the parapet to watch the take-off, a process as thoroughly impressive as the landing. Slowly increasing power, Jack tilted the helicopter forward and almost seemed to roll off the pinnacle with a single motion into the vastness of the canyon. We watched him for a moment skimming like a mayfly toward the heights of Waialeale, and then silence settled over the immense gorge.

Once we had adjusted to our surroundings—or rather, the lack of them—we began to enjoy the magnificent view. Roughly a mile away on either side of us the main walls of the canyon plunged vertically into deep recesses forever beyond reach of the sun. Against the great pool of shadow below, tiny flecks of what appeared to be dust or pollen caught the sun's rays, drifting slowly along on a faint breeze. When they turned and began to float upwind, I suddenly realized they were birds soaring hundreds of feet down in the chasm.

From a distance the canyon walls stood out sharply in colorful layers—ocher, rust, and varying shades of brown—recording an eternity of volcanic eruptions. Several of the layers contained boulders whose weathered shapes suggested the scowling faces of ancient gods surveying a vast and lonely realm. The sight brought home the fact that we were marooned high above the canyon floor, and Louise had a sobering thought.

"Suppose Jack has engine trouble on Waialeale?"

I reassured her that Jack had a second helicopter and that its pilot knew our flight plan. But I was relieved nonetheless when we caught the

Festive prints greet Santa Claus during the 1969 Christmas show at the Lihue shopping center on Kauai. Months of practice at Lihue Christian Church under the tutelage of Charles Kaneyama (right) brought the youngsters to concert readiness. "O little town . . ." sings one of the choir as she grips the ukulele.

distant whine of an engine and saw Jack approaching from far below us.

He had brought Louise a present from Waialeale, a tiny plant that gave evidence of the vast distances life has traveled over millions of years in reaching Hawaii.

"We call it sundew," Jack said, placing the fragile specimen with its bell-shaped flowers in Louise's palm. "It's a carnivore—a flycatcher of the genus *Drosera* that grows in a good many areas of the Northern Hemisphere, including Alaska." Louise, a longtime gardener, was fascinated. "How did it get here?" she asked. Jack shook his head, smiling.

"Nobody knows, but man didn't bring it; the sundew reached Hawaii long before he did. Most likely some migratory bird brought the seed in its feathers or intestines thousands, perhaps millions, of years ago. One guess would be the golden plover, since it migrates from the Arctic to the Antarctic every year by way of Hawaii." He nodded at John Sincock. "There's the expert, and even he can't say."

We forsook Kauai after that, heading out across Kaulakahi Channel toward Niihau, the "Forbidden Island." Along the way John Sincock gave us a thumbnail sketch.

"Niihau belongs to the Robinson family of Kauai," John began. "One of their ancestors, Mrs. Eliza Sinclair, bought it from Kamehameha V in 1864 for $10,000. The Sinclairs were sheep ranchers who came here from New Zealand, and there's a delightful story about the purchase.

"Kamehameha apparently liked the Sinclairs, and he originally offered them a strip of land on Oahu running from what is now downtown Honolulu all the way to Diamond Head, for $50,000. Of course the area included Waikiki, and nowadays you couldn't buy 10 feet of shoreline for that. Even then it was an unbelievable offer.

"But the Sinclairs were ranchers to the bone," John continued. "One of the sons rode out to look the land over and told his mother: 'If you buy that spread you might just as well put your $50,000 in a gunny sack and throw it in the ocean—the land won't graze five head of sheep!'"

Instead, the family bought Niihau's 73 square miles, turning it into a cattle and sheep ranch and eventually into a private refuge for pure Hawaiians, who work the ranch and who account for most of the island's 250 inhabitants. The language of Niihau is a relatively pure strain of Hawaiian, closer in some respects to an older tongue, Tahitian, than to the version that has evolved elsewhere in the 50th State. For years outsiders have been refused permission to visit the small outpost, even for such worthwhile projects as John Sincock's survey of endangered wildlife. Hence the offer by Jack, a devoted conservationist, to fly John on inspection trips now and then.

"People who know the Niihau islanders say they're wonderfully kind and gentle," Jack added, "but they certainly cling to their privacy. In 1959 when Hawaii held a plebescite on statehood, the vote was a 17-to-1 landslide in favor of it. Out of 240 districts in the territory only Niihau voted 'No.'

"Things are changing now, and a new generation of Robinsons is coming along. Niihau has some serious economic problems besides those caused by drought, but all of us are hoping the islanders will make a go

Slicing through geologic time, Waimea ("reddish water") Canyon lays bare the layer-cake pattern of lava flows that formed Kauai. Through millenniums, heavy rainfall draining from the heights onto the island's volcanic flank carved a gorge 14.5 miles long and 2,857 feet deep. To reach this view, visitors climb from hot cane fields on the lee side to cool, misty forests, refuge for rare birds.

of it." He broke off. "But here it is—welcome to the Forbidden Island."

Clearing a high rampart of barren cliffs by less than 100 feet, we skimmed across a drab landscape of yellowing range grass and tortured kiawe trees, interrupted here and there by the open wounds of erosion —raw patches of red volcanic earth. Now and then we spied a small group of sheep or cattle clustered around a shallow drinking pond.

Over one pond John made a welcome discovery in the form of some 250 graceful Hawaiian stilts, long-legged birds that exploded beneath us in a swirling black-and-white tornado. He jotted an entry in his notebook and then turned to Louise and me.

"There are probably no more than 1,500 of those birds left in the world," he said. "Like the pure Hawaiians they've dwindled to a relative few, and for many of the same reasons—loss of natural habitat and accustomed food supply, introduction of foreign diseases and competitors, and, finally, massive human indifference. Niihau has wild as well as human refugees, but time is running out on all of them."

At the island's southern tip Jack turned and followed the leeward coast north to Niihau's only real community, roughly a score of frame houses known as Puuwai—literally "heart" in Hawaiian.

Despite their voluntary isolation the islanders lived up to Jack's impression of friendliness. As we circled low over the houses, doors swung open and adults as well as children hurried out to wave. Few villages in the world are apt to ignore a low-flying helicopter, yet there was something unmistakably warm and kindly in Puuwai's reaction. We got a similar greeting from two paniolos headed north on horseback several miles from the village—this time with an eloquent flourish of ten-gallon hats.

In the end we broke Niihau's rigid kapu by landing, but only for a matter of minutes on behalf of some unknown islander. As we reached the northeastern coast Jack saw a cow entangled by the horns in a kiawe thicket, obviously in the last stages of exhaustion from a hopeless struggle. Picking a level area just back of the water's edge, he made another smooth landing and set off to investigate, declining our offers of help. Louise and John and I did a little beachcombing along the rocky shore.

I have never known a scavenger with Louise's instincts and outrageous luck; by the time Jack returned from a successful rescue mission she had retrieved two handsome green glass floats, the kind used by Japanese fishermen to buoy their nets. The sturdy globes work loose wherever the fishing fleets operate, sometimes off Japan itself, and drift thousands of miles across the Pacific to end up on Hawaii's shores as treasured finds. Jack stowed the prizes away and we took off for Kauai's Na Pali Coast, reaching the southern end of the great headland after a 10-minute flight.

Late-afternoon sun enfolded the massive cliffs, turning a score of waterfalls into rivulets of molten silver forever replenishing the bright crucible of the sea. Elsewhere the palisade had given way to the eternal rush of water, opening out in steep valleys overgrown with jungle, like patches of moss gleaming from the cracks of some giant retaining wall.

It was a scene borrowed from a *mele,* the ancient form of Hawaiian poetic chant that once took the place of written history, describing memorable events or the wonders of nature. More than likely just such a

In its cloud-shadowed valley Kauai's Hanalei River winds among glinting emerald plots of taro hemmed in by blue-green peaks. Wilbert Tai Hook (left), a fireman in the nearby village of Hanalei, wades through the rich ooze of his field with his taro harvest. Cooking and pounding will turn the potato-like roots into poi, a mild-flavored staple for native meals. Among the islands, Kauai cultivates the most taro.

view had inspired some long-ago poet to compose one of countless verses in honor of Kauai, among the most beloved of Hawaii's islands:

Serene she rests, rising from the sea
To lift the leaf-bud of her mountain . . .
To the sky—

Others, perhaps, had seen the Na Pali Coast as a symbol of hope and the end of a terrible ordeal. Many historians believe that the Polynesian discoverers of Hawaii came ashore the first time at one of the great valleys along the coast, doubtless filled with gratitude for delivery after a grueling 2,400-mile voyage across unknown seas from the Marquesas.

For a finale Jack climbed the northern edge of the rampart, soaring across the velvet green folds of Kauai's windward slope. Skirting to the east of Kawaikini volcano, we passed through the garland of mist forever draped about the heights by moisture-laden trades. Then we were out once more in sunlight, descending between banks of dazzling cumulus toward the heliport at Lihue. I thought for a moment of Casey Coryell and a day many weeks before on Oahu, for we seemed to be fluming down the clouds.

Above the reach of seismic sea waves, Kauai's Kilauea Point Light Station sends its beam 23 miles to sea to mark the island's northernmost spot.

Despite Kauai's nickname and lonely grandeur, its charm stems first of all from people, a fact that Louise and I were to discover during the days that followed. Not that anyone made a special effort; as Maile says, they're just born that way.

Maile Semitekol is district manager of the Hawaii Visitors Bureau in Lihue, the charming woman whose full first name, as she had told me earlier, means, "the small, fragrant maile vine closely entwined with the climbing ieie plant of the upland forest." Maile, however, is even more closely entwined with the life of Kauai and its inhabitants. She introduced us to a good many of them. Nowhere in Hawaii are there people more varied yet more alike in the common gift of hospitality.

There was a morning at Kokee, the National Aeronautics and Space Administration's tracking station above Waimea Canyon, with its director, Virgil True. Mr. True and his staff had recently put in an exhausting week monitoring the Apollo 11 flight and man's historic first landing on the moon, yet he generously laid aside official reports for an hour or so to conduct a tour of the station. I confess I understood a mere fraction of all we saw, but I recall that Mr. True wasn't entirely satisfied with Kokee's radar. It was only accurate down to an area five yards wide at a range of 32,000 miles, and he was looking forward to new equipment that would reduce the possible error to a more comfortable one of a single yard at 240,000 miles, the distance to the moon.

There was another dedicated scientist and friend of Maile's, Margaret Kupihea, in the town of Kapaa on Kauai's east coast. She received me cordially one afternoon in her living room, although she had been up at four o'clock in the morning. At that hour she had been diving offshore with a pair of goggles and a small knife to gather edible limpets called *'opihi,* something not every 67-year-old great-grandmother would do.

Mrs. Kupihea is a highly respected healer whose ancient craft, practiced with various minerals and herbs, has produced many authentic cures. For the most part she preferred to talk about legends of Kauai—about the *Menehune,* or little people, who perform incredible tasks overnight for deserving humans, and the *pō kāne,* or night marchers, dread souls of the departed who carry off unsuspecting mortals to eternal damnation.

When I left, however, Mrs. Kupihea assumed the healer's role. She gave me a small block of red volcanic stone called *'alaea,* with instructions on how to grind it up and swallow it in a glass of lightly salted water as a cure for stomach ailments, such as those caused by overeating. On Kauai there could hardly be a more thoughtful gift.

Keala Kinimaka's gift is less easily transmitted, though she tried to teach me a basic element or two. She is 17 years old, a student of classical hula, and an extraordinarily beautiful girl. I met her one evening at the Tahiti Longhouse, an attractive restaurant-nightclub on Poipu Beach, where she was performing for an audience of tourists with her three sisters and a gifted young teacher of hula named Henry Taese.

I had been in Hawaii long enough to distinguish between the stately classical hula and the more flamboyant popular variations offered that evening. Afterward I asked Henry and Keala why they didn't include at least a sample of the traditional form, if only for comparison. Henry answered plainly that it was a matter of dignity and good taste.

"Classical hula," he explained, "was born of the ancient Polynesian religion, and those who practice the art still consider it essentially sacred, an expression of the soul through means of the body. You would no more perform such a thing in a nightclub or restaurant than you would, let us say, celebrate a mass or present a Christmas pageant there."

Careful polishing at Kilauea Point station keeps the 4-ton clamshell lens ready to intensify its 1,000-watt lamp into a 1,400,000-candlepower beam.

It suddenly occurred to me that the only performances of traditional hula I had witnessed were at a gathering of artists in Honolulu and in a later program given by the children of Hana for a private audience of parents and friends.

"Commercial dancing is different," Keala added. "Many of the gestures we use in it are the same as those in classical hula, but they tell a different kind of story. Henry composed the routines you saw tonight, but pure hula follows the ancient meles, or chants. In school Henry teaches both types of hula, but one is art and the other is entertainment."

I asked Keala to demonstrate a few gestures used in hula. For the first she swept her hands in a graceful circle around her shoulders and head, an unmistakable representation of the moon. The second was almost as simple, consisting of hands clasped to the breast and then extended outward to symbolize the gift of one's heart.

The third gesture was more complicated, beginning with both hands joined over the left hip, then flowing upward diagonally across the body and ending in a lovely unfurling motion above the right shoulder. After a moment I gave up, and Keala smiled. "It is simple," she explained. "One climbs the mountain and finds a beautiful flower at the top." She made the gesture again. "Do you see it?"

I saw two flowers—Keala herself, and her creation.

Finally there was Maile's own family, which includes nearly half the coastal village of Hanalei. Or so it seemed the night Louise and I met them at the Semitekols' house for a farewell luau. Maile's husband Bob introduced us to them all: Uncle Barlow Chu, Aunt Jennie and Uncle Jack Saffrey, Cousin Richard Hooikaika, Uncle Ezra Pa, Cousins Dooley and David Kaaumoana, and a score of others.

None of them, it turned out, is related by blood to Maile. Instead, they are her 'umeke 'ohana, or "calabash family," the wonderful Hawaiian term for close friends who have shared many joys in life, including meals around the common bowl—or calabash in earlier days. At a full-scale luau the joys are monumental.

It took two huge tables on the lānai, or veranda, to hold the feast Maile had spread, with hardly a square inch left over. Aunt Jennie Saffrey, a marvelously ample woman and one of the contributors, took me on a short guided tour to identify some of the delicacies: boiled mūhe'e, or cuttlefish; salted salmon sprinkled with onions and kneaded in the style known as lomilomi; chicken steamed with vegetables; diced and pickled aku, or skipjack; beef simmered in fresh tomatoes; marinated 'ō'io, the delicate bonefish; chilled crab; freshwater shrimp; and 'opihi, the highly prized raw limpets. In addition there was an assortment of mangoes, avocados, slices of fresh coconut, candied ginger, macadamia and kukui nuts, two of Aunt Jennie's miraculous coconut cakes, several consistencies of poi, and of course my old friend, pua'a, the traditional pig.

Uncle Jack and Aunt Jennie had attended to the pua'a at home, dividing the carcass into individual servings and wrapping them in lū'au—tender young leaves of the taro plant that have come to symbolize the feast itself. Adding an outer layer of ti leaves, they had steamed the packets for hours in an imu, or underground oven heated with glowing rocks.

It had all the dimensions of a Roman orgy, and I questioned whether we would ever make a dent in it.

"Don't you worry, now," Aunt Jennie assured me cheerfully, "we'll just settle down and sing our way through it."

And so we did, with Cousin David Kaaumoana on the guitar, Cousin Dooley on the washtub bass, and several ukuleles that changed hands as nimbly as the translation of their name—"leaping flea"—suggests.

The music was even more varied and spectacular than the food, though always in the soft melodic style of Hawaii that combines joy with a strain of eternal sadness. Maile's beautifully clear soprano led a dozen voices in the melody, gliding rather than shifting between notes in the way of

Tahiti Nui bar in Hanalei mixes patrons and music with a dash of laughter. A washtub bass adds vibrant tones, deepening as the clothesline slackens. Ukuleles pass from hand to hand and song begins when friends get together.

Granddaughter of missionaries, Miss Mabel Wilcox reads the bound letters of Abner and Lucy Wilcox at Waioli Mission, where the couple taught the Lord's word, along with useful skills. They came to Hanalei in 1846, bringing New England furnishings and strong Protestantism. Religious fervor faded in the 1860's, but the mission house remains as a testament to an enduring faith.

island singing. Aunt Jennie proved an even more gifted contralto than cook, leading others in rich and intricate harmony.

They sang of Hanalei, of the crescent harbor that gives the village its name, and of Kauai, "where the sun rises and sets again, where the surf ... curves and bends." There were songs of the other islands, where "the lapping of the sea is gentle, the fragrance of seaweed is in the air," and one memorable ballad called *Kaula 'Ili,* "The Lasso," describing a cowboy on a hill who is told by the birds what a lovely day it is to ride up into the high mountains.

As Aunt Jennie predicted, the feast gradually melted away, for instruments continued to pass from hand to hand and the performers took time out, drifting to the tables along with the singers. Uncle Barlow and I sampled the pua'a together and found it delicious. We moved on to the poi, the mixture of ground taro root with water that is a staple in the islands, especially the rural areas.

Uncle Barlow is an authority on poi and he told me about some of the other uses to which Hawaiians put it besides food—a gentle cleansing agent, a cure for colic in small children, an antidote for scorpion and bee sting, and a soothing poultice for eye and skin irritations. I remarked that mainlanders often dismiss poi as barely edible library paste, and Uncle Barlow surprised me by nodding.

"They are wrong about flavor, but right about the paste," he said. "When I was a boy I put all my school scrapbooks together with poi, and they haven't come apart yet. It was wonderful for building kites, too, though you could be in big trouble if it rained."

Long after midnight Louise and I said goodbye, and Maile kissed us each in farewell aloha. "Now you have an 'umeke 'ohana on Kauai," she said, "and that means you will come back one day."

I suspect we will, for as we took off early the next morning for Honolulu, Louise glanced back a final time at the island's green silhouette and said happily, "That's what I call a calabash home."

There was one last corner of the 50th State to visit—the Northwestern Hawaiian Islands, or Leewards, older still than Kauai but clothed in none of her gentle magic. Bleak and forbidding, the score or so of weathered pinnacles, atolls, and islets stretch some 1,200 miles northwest of Kauai, separated one from another by vast reaches of empty Pacific. Together they add little more than three square miles to Hawaii's land area.

Even the sturdy Polynesians of the past found the Northwestern islands too grim for permanent settlement. One or two of the larger shelter the forlorn ruins of villages fashioned of volcanic stone and then abandoned under the relentless pressure of hunger or drought. Most of the island names are distinctly un-Hawaiian—Gardner Pinnacles, French Frigate Shoals, and the islands known as Necker, Laysan, and Lisianski.

Where man has met with meager success other creatures flourish. The Northwestern islands constitute one of the world's foremost nesting grounds for seabirds, an area protected since 1909 by federal law as the Hawaiian Islands National Wildlife Refuge.

Of the Northwestern chain only remote Kure Island, just outside the refuge, is normally accessible, thanks to a U. S. Coast Guard navigational

Catching the surge, Nick Beck, vice-principal of Hanalei School, handles his catamaran like a surfboard. Coral studs Hanalei Bay, and currents make the sailing tricky. But the catamaran, like the double-hulled canoe of Hawaiian chiefs, skims above reefs lying only inches below the surface. At right, Beck checks over his craft before launching.

aid station on the tiny atoll. The U. S. Navy supports the 24-man unit from its own base on the Midway Islands, a pair of larger atolls 52 miles to the east and belonging neither to the wildlife refuge nor to the State of Hawaii but to the Navy itself. The Navy agreed to fly me from Honolulu to Midway aboard one of its biweekly commercial contract flights and from there to Kure by supply flight in an amphibian.

Despite the presence of Navy families on Midway, women visitors are politely discouraged, so Louise and I parted in Honolulu, she for the mainland and I for a visit to the last outpost of the Hawaiian chain.

The three-hour flight from Honolulu spanned roughly 1,300 miles of ocean and seven million years in the life of Hawaii. Heading northwest from Oahu, we passed progressively older islands in the chain, ending with the veterans, Midway and Kure. The latter is believed to have emerged from the sea some 10.5 million years ago.

In the ageless battle with the elements both Midway and Kure have suffered monumental defeat, representing the mere remnants of once mighty peaks now flattened to within a few yards of the ocean's restless surface and braced for the final assault behind outthrust shields of encircling coral. Looking down on Midway, I could visualize the entire Northwestern chain as a vast graveyard of islands returning over incalculable time to the sea that gave them birth.

I found Midway's 2,150 military and civilian residents braced for their own familiar kind of assault, the annual return of more than half a million albatrosses—the famous gooney birds of Midway—from a long sojourn at sea to the tumultuous business of nesting. Typical of Midway's forbearance under the massive invasion of its two square miles is the island's regulation that gooney birds have squatter's rights on the golf course. Thus, if a player encounters a bird taking its ease on the green between himself and the cup he must move the ball, not the gooney.

A far more serious hazard, one that the Navy still faces despite considerable research and expense, is the occasional collision between gooney birds and planes over Midway's airstrips. Happily for Lt. (jg.) Charles Leo and me, the runway was clear the afternoon we took off for Kure in a Grumman HU-16 amphibian, an aircraft appropriately designated "Albatross." Within 20 minutes we were letting down toward Kure, a narrow crescent of white sand set in the tranquil blue of the Pacific like a quarter-moon against a late-afternoon sky.

Virtually all of the island's 24 Coast Guardsmen met us at the apron to unload mail and supplies. We had barely an hour's ground time before the return flight to Midway. Jef Kaiser, Kure's 23-year-old medical corpsman, took me on a short jeep tour of the island's one-third square mile.

We began at the main buildings beneath a 625-foot-high antenna for LORAN—Long Range Aid to Navigation—by which Kure guides ships and aircraft between Hawaii and the *(Continued on page 198)*

Overleaf: Dizzying rampart of Kauai's Na Pali Coast suggests the paws of a colossal sphinx. Sheer-sided valleys, perhaps the first landfall of Polynesians, hold remains of their settlements. With lines set, a sampan fisherman watches for the flurry of birds that betrays fish feeding near the sea's surface.

PAUL B. KRAUS (BELOW) AND N. PHILIP WATTERSON, JR.

From the air, Midway's Eastern Island (foreground) and Sand Island wear a sea-washed reef lei. Lying next to the Hawaiian Islands National Wildlife Refuge, U.S.-owned Midway serves as a base for sea-air rescue and mid-ocean medical emergency services. Each October gooney birds (albatrosses) invade Midway, returning from ocean wanderings to breed and nest. Hurtling to earth, the feathered projectiles set up brooding stations without regard for runways, roads, or the 2,150 human beings under Navy command. At left, birds command the ground near the main hangar on 1,055-acre Sand Island. Tireless in flight, the grounded gooney has a seaman's rolling gait. At far left, a nesting bird provokes delighted squeals from one of Midway's youngest sailors.

western Pacific. From there Jef headed for the island's northeastern tip across scrub-carpeted land alive with roosting birds—shearwaters, sanderlings, petrels, terns, frigate birds, and a few early arrivals among the albatrosses. For all their color and animation they seemed a poor substitute for human company. I asked Jef how the average Coast Guardsman got along on Kure.

"It helps if you like wildlife and things like reef diving," he answered, "but we've got a good group and everybody finds something to keep him interested, so a year's duty manages to pass.

"I'm from Florida," he added, "and I could spend half my time here in the water, just watching things like that." He waved at a shapeless brown blob ahead of us at the water's edge that suddenly shuffled to life as we approached and hunched its way into the sea.

"That's a monk seal," Jef said. "There are only about a thousand of them left in the islands now. They've got all the grace of a 500-pound sack of meal on land, but they're plain poetry underwater."

We followed the island's southern strip of beach toward the west. At one spot Jef pointed to a patch of sand stained dark brown. "Now and then something happens here that everybody gets involved in," he said. "The other day a young bottle-nosed whale washed ashore, injured and dying, and more than 30 sharks followed it in. I have some shark hooks from Florida and we got some quarter-inch nylon line and chunks of raw meat and caught over two dozen of them, including a 14-foot tiger shark."

Our hour was soon up, and Jef delivered me to the airstrip. I thanked him and climbed into the Grumman with Lieutenant Leo and a young Coast Guardsman bound for Midway and a day or two off duty.

Not everyone on Kure, it seems, objects to the solitude of Hawaii's remote western outpost. During the flight back to Midway the young Coast Guardsman explained that a year's tour of duty on Kure usually entitles a man to his preference for a next post. He had only a month left to go on the island, and I asked what he had put in for after that.

"I'd like a change of scene," he said, "and a little colder climate, so I asked for Attu, Alaska." He beamed. "I understand it's been approved."

My time in Hawaii was running out and I caught the next plane to Honolulu, planning on a flight to the mainland the next day. As we left the Northwestern chain behind and began our descent for Oahu, I caught a distant glimpse of Kauai and the Na Pali Coast to the south.

There, perhaps, it had all begun, more than 1,200 years ago, with the landing by a handful of courageous seafarers who had challenged the unknown and triumphed over it. They had changed the course of history throughout the Pacific and in lands far beyond. Those who came after them are doing the same—adding their energy, their vision, and their great concern for mankind to a constantly changing and, one may hope, improving world.

It is as though Hawaiians in their gentle fashion are forever driven by a command implicit in the lines from an ancient Polynesian mele:

> *Go on over the deep blue ocean,*
> *And shake the foundations of heaven.*

"Niihau glitters in the calm," chanted the ancients of the craggy island in the distance beyond Kauai. Privately held, closed to tourists, its dry slopes yield a frugal living to a few hundred Hawaiians — remnant of the "very peaceable & friendly" people Captain Cook found in 1778. Since then, Hawaii has welcomed change, but Niihau — the "Forbidden Island" — remains tuned to the past.

INDEX

Illustrations references, including legends, appear in *italics*

Additional references

The reader may wish to refer to the following NATIONAL GEOGRAPHIC articles: John W. Aldrich, "The Gooney Birds of Midway," June 1964; Jim Becker, "Look What's Happened to Honolulu," October 1969; Deena Clark, "The Flowers That Say 'Aloha,' " January 1967; Thomas J. Hargrave, "Photographing A Volcano in Action," October 1955; J. R. Magness, "How Fruit Came to America," September 1951; S. Dillon Ripley, "Saving the Nene, World's Rarest Goose," November 1965; Frederick Simpich, Jr., "Because It Rains on Hawaii," November 1949; "Fountain of Fire in Hawaii (Kilauea Iki Crater)," March 1960; "Hawaii, U.S.A.," July 1960; "Honolulu, Mid-Ocean Capital," May 1954; James A. Sugar, "Starfish Threaten Pacific Reefs," March 1970; Paul A. Zahl, "Unsung Beauties of Hawaii's Coral Reefs," October 1959; "Volcanic Fires of the 50th State: Hawaii National Park," June 1959; "Face and Floor of the 'Peaceful Sea,' " October 1969; "Watery Hawaii: Fiftieth State Spans 1,600 Miles of Ocean," July 1960.

Composition for *Hawaii* by National Geographic's Phototypographic Division,
John E. McConnell, Manager. Printed and bound by Fawcett Printing Corp.,
Rockville, Md. Color separations by Beck Engraving Co., Philadelphia, Pa.;
Colorgraphics, Inc., Beltsville, Md.; Graphic Color Plate, Inc., Stamford, Conn.;
Graphic South, Inc., Charlotte, N.C.; The Lanman Co., Alexandria, Va.; Lebanon
Valley Offset, Inc., Cleona, Pa.; and Progressive Color Corp., Rockville, Md.